Hodder Cambridge Primary

English

Learner's Book
Stage 6

Moira Brown
Series Editor: Dr John Bennett

HODDER
EDUCATION
AN HACHETTE UK COMPANY

The Publishers would like to thank the following for permission to reproduce copyright material:

Acknowledgements

p11, from *The Eagle Trail* written by Robert Rigby, text © 2014 Robert Rigby, reproduced by permission of Walker Books Ltd., London SE11 5HJ, *www.walker.co.uk*; p11, adapted from *A Boaster Beaten* from *Crossing the Line and Other Stories, Reader E* (Hodder Education); p20, adapted from *The Biography of Roald Dahl* at *About.com (http://childrensbooks.about.com/ authorsillustrato/a/roalddahl.html)*; p26, from *Boy: Tales of Childhood* by Roald Dahl, published by Johnathan Cape Ltd and Penguin Books Ltd and reproduced with permission; p24, extract from Roald Dahl biography from *About.com* Children's Books; p32, from *The Diary of Samuel Pepys* by Samuel Pepys (1633-1703); p33 from *My Story: Workhouse*, text copyright © Pamela Oldfield, 2004. Reproduced by permission of Scholastic Ltd. All rights reserved; p34, from *Diary of a Wimpy Kid* by Jeff Kinney (first published in the US by Harry N. Abrams 2007, Puffin Books 2008) copyright © Jeff Kinney and reproduced by permission; p48, from *Tom's Midnight Garden* by Philippa Pearce (OUP, 2008), copyright © Oxford University Press 1958, reproduced by permission of Oxford University Press; p50, adapted from *www.endangeredspecie.com/Ways_To_Help.htm*; p62, adapted from *The Giant Okab* by Shirin Adl and Elizabeth Laird, from *Pea Boy and Other Stories* by Elizabeth Laird, published by Frances Lincoln Ltd, copyright © 2009 Reproduced by permission of Francis Lincoln Ltd; p65, 121 words from *Goodnight Mister Tom* by Michelle Magorian, published by Puffin 2010. Copyright © Michelle Magorian, 1981; p66-67, from *Frost Hollow Hall* by Emma Carroll, published by Faber and Faber; p72, *A Narrow Escape and Other Stories, Reader D* (Hodder Education), adapted from *The Hermit who was a Hypocrite* from *Tales Told in India* by Berta Metzger, by permission of the author and Oxford University Press (Indian Branch-Mumbai); p76, from *The Midnight Zoo* by Sonya Hannett, text © 2010 Sonya Hannett and reproduced by permission of Walker Books Ltd. London SE11 5HJ, *www.walker.co.uk*; p82, adapted from *Anansi and the Moss-covered Rock* from *Caribbean Comprehension Book Six* (Hodder Education); from *Almost a Disaster* from *Crossing the Line and Other Stories, Reader E* (Hodder Education); from *The Secret Garden* by Frances Hodgson Burnett (d.1910); p82, from *The Animals of Farthing Wood* by Colin Dann text copyright © 1979 Colin Dann, published by Egmont UK Ltd and used with permission; from *The Happy Prince* by Oscar Wilde published by Puffin Classics; p84, from *Kensuke's Kingdom* by Michael Morpurgo, published by Egmont UK Ltd and used with permission; p94, from *Bella's Den* by Berlie Doherty published by Egmont UK Ltd and used with permission; p98, *Silver* by Walter de la Mare (1873-1956) used with permission of The Literary Trustees of Walter de la Mare and The Society of Authors as their representative; p102, *The Whistling Wind*, © 1980, Wang Xiaoni © Translation 2004, revisions by Simon Patton ©, used with permission from Poetry International; p102, *The Wind* by Christina Rossetti (1830-1894); p104–105, *The Listeners* by Walter de la Mare (1873-1956) used with permission of The Literary Trustees of Walter de la Mare and The Society of Authors as their representative; p112, *Song of a Blue Mountain Stream* by Reginald M. Murray from *Crossing the Line and Other Stories, Reader E* (Hodder Education); p113, from *The Poetry of Robert Frost* by Robert Frost, published by Jonathan Cape. Reprinted by permission of The Random House Group Ltd; p113, *Fog* by Carl Sandburg; p120–121, from *Little House on the Prairie* by Laura Ingalls Wilder, published by HarperCollins; p126, *Snow Leopard advert* reproduced by permission of WWF-UK; p131, adapted from *Coraline* by Neil Gaiman, © Neil Gaiman 2003, published by Bloomsbury Publishing Plc and used with permission; p133, extract from *Swami and Friends*, from *Malgudi Omnibus* by R.K. Narayan, published by Vintage Classics. Reproduced by permission of The Random House Group Ltd; p137, extract from *Shadow of the Minotaur* by Alan Gibbons, published by Dolphin; p141, from *The Man with the Yellow Face* by Anthony Horowitz, published by Hachette Children's Books.

Every effort has been made to trace all copyright holders, but if any have been inadvertently overlooked the Publishers will be pleased to make the necessary arrangements at the first opportunity.

Practice Test exam-style questions and sample answers are written by the author.

Although every effort has been made to ensure that website addresses are correct at time of going to press, Hodder Education cannot be held responsible for the content of any website mentioned in this book. It is sometimes possible to find a relocated web page by typing in the address of the home page for a website in the URL window of your browser.

Hachette UK's policy is to use papers that are natural, renewable and recyclable products and made from wood grown in well-managed forests and other sustainable sources. The logging and manufacturing processes are expected to conform to the environmental regulations of the country of origin.

Orders: Please conatct Hachette UK Distribution, Hely Hutchinson Centre, Milton Road, Didcot, Oxforshire, OX11 7HH. Telephone: +44 (0)1235 827827. Email education@hachette.co.uk. Lines are open from 9 a.m. to 5 p.m., Monday to Friday. You can also order through our website: www.hoddereducation.com

© Moira Brown 2015
First published in 2015 by
Hodder Education,
An Hachette UK Company
Carmelite House
50 Victoria Embankment
London EC4Y 0DZ

Impression number   10 9
Year   2021

Cover illustration by Sandy Lightley
Illustrations by Marleen Visser
Typeset in Swissforall in 12pt by Resolution
Printed and bound by CPI Group (UK) Ltd, Croydon CR0 4YY

A catalogue record for this title is available from the British Library

ISBN 978 1471 830204

Contents

Looking closer at non-fiction

I know and understand the features of different non-fiction texts.

Helpful hints

Non-fiction texts have their own set of language features, organisation and layout. There is a big difference between an advertisement persuading adults to buy soap powder, and an explanation text for school children!

1 Copy the table below and identify the correct non-fiction type. Use this list to help for: **instructions, letter, newspaper report, diary, biography, advertisement.**

Extract	Non-fiction type
a Take one shoelace in each hand and make the shape of a cross.	
b Come to 'High Hopes' adventure theme park for the experience of a lifetime!	
c Schoolboy in Dramatic Rescue of Teacher!	
d Micah called up about three in the morning, to tell us of a great fire they saw in the city. So I rose, and went to the window.	
e William Shakespeare was born in Stratford-upon-Avon in Warwickshire, and baptised a few days later on 26 April 1564.	
f Dear Sir, I am writing to complain about an item of clothing I purchased at your store.	

2 Identify which non-fiction type uses the language features listed below. Choose from **Persuasion (P), Instructions (I), Argument (A)**

a Imperative verbs at the start of sentences, for example, *Take, Cut*
b Connectives which explain points, for example, *although, in contrast*
c Adjectives and adverbs used for emotive effect, for example, *stupendous, brilliantly*
d Personal pronouns which include the reader, for example, *you, we, our*
e Title sometimes put forward as a question, for example, *Should school be made compulsory?*
f Connectives used to indicate chronology (time), for example, *Next … Then … When …*
g Sound features, for example, alliteration, rhythm, onomatopoeia, rhyme
h Conclusion shown by words and phrases, for example, *In conclusion… Finally*
i Encouraging remarks, for example, *Just four easy steps to …*

Comparison of the language, style and impact of non-fiction texts

1 Recount texts re-tell the story of something that has happened. Read the three recount extracts shown.

a What text types are A, B and C?

b Give three similarities and three differences between the three texts.

A **Monday**

Boring morning in school! Maths was SO hard! At break, played with Henry. Had chips and salad for lunch. PE (cricket) in the afternoon, and our side won. Hooray! Yucky stew for dinner, then attempted maths homework. Couldn't finish it. Watched some TV. In bed by 9pm.

B Pamela Mordecai was born in 1942 in Kingston, Jamaica. She is a Jamaican teacher, scholar, poet and writer of short fiction. She attended high school in Jamaica and college in the USA, where she did a degree in English. Mordecai has written over thirty books including children's books and five books of poetry for adults.

C

Lorry Error Engulfs City in Bubbles!

Yesterday, an error by a lorry driver caused the main street in Cairo to be covered in bubbles. When attempting to reverse his lorry, Abdul Serai accidentally discharged 5000 litres of 'Happy Dishes' washing-up liquid on to the street. Abdul said, "Everyone was shouting directions, and I suddenly became confused. I'm afraid I pressed the release button instead of the reverse."

Talk Partners

Choose **one** of the three texts. What tips would you give to a younger class on how to write this type of text? Share your tips with a talk partner.

List all the non-fiction text types that have been focused upon so far. Can you think of any others not yet mentioned? Agree on a list with a partner. (Hint: letter, article)

Try this

Meanings of connectives

Helpful hints

Connectives – which can be words or phrases – are very useful in non-fiction texts for putting ideas in order and linking them. They can be used to connect ideas between sentences, or make links between paragraphs.

Here are some examples of different types of connectives. Notice how they can be a word or a phrase.

Adding points	Ordering points	Reinforcing points
also	first of all	besides this
furthermore	next	this proves
moreover	finally	increasingly
Explaining points	**Contrasting points**	**Summming up points**
for example	however	as a result
in other words	on the other hand	thanks to this
that meant	but	therefore

1 Write about what you did yesterday. Your aim is to use at least eight of the connectives from the list above.

For example, *'First of all I got up, dressed and had a shower ...'*

2 Connectives can be placed at the **start** of a sentence – and **inside** it. Pick out the connectives used in this short article about drones. Find at least six!

Tiny, unmanned aircraft are being used more and more for a huge variety of tasks, but landing drones safely has proved to be a problem.

Now one researcher has designed a pair of legs that can be attached to drones. These will allow them to grab on to the surfaces – for example, branches or phone lines. Moreover, the 'claws' on the legs are sharp, therefore enabling a really tight grip. This also means the drone has time to do things – such as shut down its engines, or even fully recharge.

Although drones were first used by researchers working in remote areas, they are being used increasingly to find survivors in places hit by natural disasters.

I can use a wide range of connectives to make the relationship between ideas clear.

I can use connectives to structure an argument or discussion.

I can vary vocabulary, expression and tone of voice to engage the listener.

More connectives

1

a Write two paragraphs on what you would do if you were in charge of the country for a day. What would you change, and why?

- The first paragraph could be about the school or the town where you live.
- The second paragraph could be about the whole country – or even the whole world! Remember to use connectives to link your ideas.
- Your ideas will sound more convincing if you back them up in some way. For example:

Firstly, I would like to change the school day, so that we have more free time. **At present,** we do not have enough. **The result of this** is that we are made to work too hard, and get tired. **Eventually,** learning suffers – particularly in the afternoon. **Secondly ...**

Notice how:
- the first sentence makes clear what should be changed
- the second sentence introduces the argument
- the third and fourth sentences back up the argument.

b When you have finished, underline the words you think are important. These might include some connectives.

Talk Partners

Read your ideas aloud to a partner. Emphasise the words underlined; hold your body up straight – and enunciate the consonants and vowels in each word. A clear, well presented talk will make your argument seem more convincing!

How to spell connectives

Helpful hints

Here are some tips on remembering how to spell words – including connectives.

- Look at the word. Cover it. Write it. Check it.
- Split the word into syllables. For example, *lat-er; in-ter-est-ed; fright-en-ing*.
- Find a word within a word. For example, *never-the-less; bus-i-ness; fav-our-ite*.
- Apply the spelling rule. For example, addition of the suffix **ly** to a word ending in 'l' as in 'finally'.
- Highlight a particular letter or letters. For example, *conse**qu**ently; i**s**land; dou**b**t*.
- Break the word into affixes. For example, un+fortunate+ly.
- Link with word families. For example, *certain, certainly, uncertain*.
- Use a mnemonic such as in *ne**c**e**ss**ary*

  = *one collar, two sleeves.*

Keep a spelling log or journal. Make a record of:

- ✓ words you need, or wish, to learn
- ✓ rules and words which show an example of a rule
- ✓ reminders and mnemonics
- ✓ key words that are difficult
- ✓ common prefixes and suffixes such as **im**, **re**, **un**, **il** and **ful**, **hood**
- ✓ ways to remember words.

1 These words are commonly misspelled. What strategies would you use to remember them?

argument	definite
successful	surprise
sincerely	embarrassed
persuade	interesting
beginning	disappointing

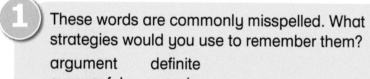

Spelling:
sincerely
embarrassed

2 Keep your own spelling journal, and organise it so that it helps you learn and remember spellings. Use some of the tips given above.

I can control and manage complex sentences.

I can use punctuation accurately and effectively in complex sentences.

Complex sentences

Helpful hints

A **complex sentence** contains a main and a subordinate clause,

'I will help you to your seat, if you come with me.'
     main clause   subordinate clause

The main clause can make sense on its own.
The subordinate clause is introduced by a subordinating connective (if) and needs the main clause in order to make complete sense. A subordinate clause must have a verb (come).

1 Using the table below, form four complex sentences. Start with the main clause, then choose an appropriate connective and clause.

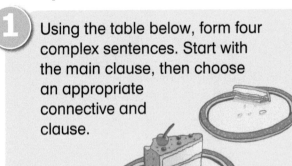

Main clause	Connective	Subordinate clause
There are no sandwiches left	if	you take me to the party.
I will come	so	I think I'll stay in.
I could not eat the food	although	it was inedible.
My favourite TV programme is on tonight	because	there is some cake.

2 Complex sentences can also begin with a subordinate clause. When this happens, notice how a comma has been used to separate the main clause from the subordinate clause.

I ran to get ready when I saw you coming.
    main clause   subordinate clause

When I saw you coming, I ran to get ready.
    subordinate clause   main clause

a Write two complex sentences which start with a main clause followed by a subordinate clause, using the connectives: **as, although.**

b Write four complex sentences which begin with the connectives: **if, since, when, to.**

Finite and non-finite verbs

> I can use punctuation accurately and effectively in complex sentences.

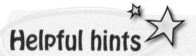
Helpful hints

A **clause** has to have a **verb**. Verbs which can stand on their own, and are able to be changed into the past and present tense are known as **finite**. Verbs which cannot stand on their own or shift tense are known as **non-finite**.

Examples of finite verbs
Isaq **plays** football.
I **spoke** German on holiday.
I **ran** all the way to school.

Examples of non-finite verbs
It took courage to **continue** up the mountain.
Going home was such a relief.
Please leave when **asked**.
Non-finite verbs will be:
 • a present participle ending in -ing
 • a past participle ending in -en, -t, -ed.

1 Beginning sentences with a non-finite clause can make them more interesting to read. For example:

Walking quickly, Senara hoped she would not miss the train.
non-finite clause   finite clause

In a, b, c write the two sentences as one sentence starting with a non-finite verb. Remember to mark off the non-finite clause with a comma.
 a   The boys ran across the playground. They were shouting loudly. *(Shouting ...)*
 b   The wind was blowing fiercely. It made it difficult to sail the boat. *(Blowing ...)*
 c   The girl slipped. She was running too fast. *(Running ...)*

2 Write a sentence using each of these non-finite clauses at the beginning.
 a   Encouraged by the boy's answer, ...
 b   Hidden in a secret cupboard, ...
 c   To manage this, ...

Commas in complex sentences

1 Re-write these complex sentences putting the commas in the correct place.

a If, you come to my party I will be really pleased.

b By running, very quickly I just made the train.

c Loaded with shopping I could barely, climb up the stairs.

2 Re-write these two extracts from texts inserting the missing commas.

a For a moment Paul was unsure what to do. He cut the bike's engine climbed off the machine and rested it against the railings.

Slowly he walked to the gates and tried the handle. They were locked. Glancing around he realised the street was deserted too as though everyone had shut themselves away behind closed doors. *(Five commas missing)*

From *The Eagle Trail* by Robert Rigby

b Away in the far and frozen north amid the ice and snow of Greenland there lived a boy named Katerparsuk. Unfortunately he had lost both his father and mother and the members of his tribe paid little attention to him. Knowing that he was dependent on his relatives the boy tried to make himself as useful as possible and so pay back what kindness was shown to him.

From *A Boaster Beaten, Crossing the Line and other stories Reader E*

Re-write the sentence below and put in the commas.

As I am sure we would all agree Adina Liberman who is the youngest girl in the school deserves first prize.

Try this

A newspaper report

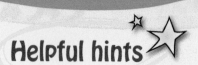
Here is how a newspaper report works.

The headline gives a snappy overview of the story. Features such as rhyme, alliteration, similes, emotive words or a rhetorical question are often used. This is to grab the reader's attention, and hook them in.

Deadly Cat Calamity
Want to Control Your Dreams?
Bats Bounce Back
Not Too Cool For School

The first paragraph will give a basic one sentence summary of the story.

Cat owners are being warned about a disease that has claimed the lives of 16 cats in the last month.

The second paragraph will start to drop in some more detail about 'who, where, what, when, why, how'.

This mystery disease causes lesions (a sore or cut) on the legs, paws and face of the cat, with these often appearing after being outside. Vets have reported an increase in the number of cases: the disease has already claimed the lives of 16 cats in the last few months.

The third paragraph will often have a comment from someone involved in the story. This is often put forward as 'direct speech'. For example, *Chief Vet, Dr Alan Cloutier said, "I would urge pet owners to keep an eye out for any unexpected cuts or sores."* Alternatively, it can be indirect or reported speech, *"Chief Vet, Doctor Alan Cloutier told us that pet owners should keep an eye out for any unexpected cuts or sores ..."*

Comments like this are used from people involved in the story because they give the reader more information about the event. They also make the story seem true!

The next few paragraphs will fill out the story with more detail of 'who, where, what, when, why, how'.

Most of the cats affected have been in the south of France, with most of the deaths close to the Var region between Toulon and St Tropez. Seven cats have been affected in other parts of the country – including Paris, Marseille, Lyon and Nantes.

The final paragraph will end the story by referring to the future, and give other examples of a similar incident or event.

Posters have been put across France warning cat owners about the disease. Vet Gustav Hautain-Nelis said there are similarities to a disease called Alabama Rot which was first reported in America in the 1980s. However, this has not yet been confirmed.

1

a   Make up another headline for the article. Remember to use some features which will get the reader's attention and make them read the story.

b   Comments from a vet have been included. Who else might the reporter have interviewed?

c   Give examples of three photographs that could have been used in the report.

Talk Partners

Take on the parts of a reporter and the owner of the cat with the disease and carry out an interview. The answers of the cat owner could then be used in the newspaper report!

Sinking Feeling

A teenager certainly had a sinking feeling when her car was swallowed by a giant sinkhole!

Nineteen-year-old Zoe Smith had parked her Volkswagen Lupo on the driveway of her parents' house in High Wycombe – as she did every evening after returning home from work. However, in the morning, she found her car had completely disappeared into a nine metre deep hole which had suddenly appeared overnight.

Zoe's mother said, "It just swallowed the car whole. The car had not only rotated and turned on its side, but was also facing the opposite direction from where it was originally parked. Zoe was in hysterics. It didn't dawn on us what had happened until about an hour later."

Although Zoe told us she was absolutely devastated at having lost her car, her mum and dad say they feel 'so lucky' that Zoe was not hurt.

The family has been told not to sleep in their home amid fears of further subsidence. Fire-fighters have placed a cordon around the hole and given safety advice to the family and the neighbourhood.

Sinkholes are extremely rare in the UK. They are caused by a collapse of earth beneath the surface. Although it is not yet known what caused this sinkhole, heavy rain or flooding is known to trigger one. No other sinkholes have been reported. ■

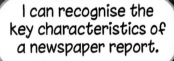

I can recognise the key characteristics of a newspaper report.

Features of newspaper

1 Read through the newspaper report on page 14.
Write the answers to these questions.

a Which language feature does the headline use to attract the reader's attention?

b Copy and complete this table. Write down what is found out about:

Who is in the story?	
When did the story happen?	
Where did the story happen?	
What happened in the story?	
How did the story end?	

c Find and copy a short quotation from the report which shows an example of:
  • direct speech
  • reported speech.

d Find and copy an example of:
  • punctuation used for effect
  • an adverb used for effect
  • a synonym for Zoe Smith
  • a synonym for Mr and Mrs Smith.

e Look at the last paragraph. Write down the two sentences which will prevent the readers from panicking.

2 The report refers to Zoe having a 'sinking feeling'. In light of what happened to the car, how is this phrase amusing?

Did you know?

In 2007, a sinkhole 150m deep and 20m wide swallowed 20 homes in Guatemala City.

In 2011, a huge sinkhole appeared overnight on a road in Beijing, swallowing a truck just after its driver and passenger escaped.

Teenager Battles Through Freezing Conditions to Set South Pole Record!

An Argentinian teenager has battled though extreme temperatures to become the youngest person to reach the South Pole after a **gruelling** 700 mile journey.

Tomás Diaz, 16, from Mendoza, spent almost 50 days on ice, skiing for an average of eight hours a day and battling temperatures as low as −50°C (−58°F) with winds of 120mph.

His father, Franco Diaz, said Tomás had set off on the final day of the trek "really motivated to make it – but it was −50°C, the coldest day so far, with really ferocious winds". The conditions were so bad that Tomás's **final leg** of the trek to the South Pole took a few hours longer than expected.

But on Saturday night, Tomás was celebrating his achievement by eating his first real meal in nearly seven weeks – **choripán**! He called his parents and told them he had reached his goal, and was now enjoying the luxury of a heated tent. He told us, "I'm really happy, but mostly relieved that for the first time in 48 days I don't have to get up tomorrow and drag my sled for nine hours in the snow and icy wind. Today was really hard, as the closer I got to the Pole, the slower I went. My legs had had enough."

Tomás is two years younger than the current world record holder, Canadian Sarah McNair-Landry, who completed the trek in 2005. Once back in Argentina, Tomás will recommence his studies as normal at school. His next challenge will be his examinations!

Glossary

choripán: sausage and salsa in crusty bread
final leg: last part
gruelling: exhausting and demanding

The styles and conventions of journalism

 Read the newspaper report on page 16 and answer the following questions.

a Facts and figures are given in newspaper reports. Copy and complete the table and explain what the numbers refer to in the report. The first one has been done for you.

Number used in report	What it refers to
700	The length of the journey Tomás made to the South Pole – 700 miles
50	
16	
48	
120	

b Copy and complete the table and summarise the purpose of each paragraph. The first one has been done for you.

Paragraph 1	Gives a one sentence summary of the story.
Paragraph 2	
Paragraph 3	
Paragraph 4	
Paragraph 5	

c Suggest a sub-heading for each of paragraphs 2 and 3. These sub-headings should inform the reader what each paragraph is about.

2 Tomás is a very determined and brave young man. Explain how these words from paragraph 1 show this.

battled   extreme   gruelling

3 Why has an exclamation mark been used at the end of this sentence?
'But on Saturday night, Tomás was celebrating his achievement by eating his first real meal in nearly seven weeks – choripán!'

4 Suggest another headline for the newspaper report.

Writing a newspaper report

1 You are going to write a newspaper report.

    a Choose one of the stories below.

- A large hole suddenly appears in a main road.
- A lorry spills its load, for example, fish, chickens, milk, oil.
- A schoolboy/girl rescues a science teacher from a burning school.
- A young person sets a record, for example, climbing a mountain, swimming across seas, walking a great distance.

    b Brainstorm your ideas for the report. Copy the diagram opposite and fill in your ideas using the questions.

2 Copy the table below and structure your ideas using this paragraph plan.

Headline
Paragraph 1: A one sentence summary of the story.
Paragraph 2: Summary repeated but with a little more detail of whom, where, when, what dropped in – but not too much. You want the reader to keep reading to find out more!
Paragraph 3: A comment from someone involved in the story.
Paragraph 4: More detail about the story – who, when, where, what, why, how.
Paragraph 5: Bring the story to an end, but also refer to the future.
Paragraph 6: Other examples of similar events. This will put the event in proportion for the reader.

I can write a newspaper report which uses the styles and conventions of journalism.

I can pay close attention to what is said, asking and answering questions to introduce new ideas.

Talk Partners

Read your paragraph plan from page 18 to a partner, and ask them to give feedback. Be ready to accept any good suggestions!

Writing presentation

Write your newspaper report using the paragraph plan. When it is finished, use the list below to ensure you have included all the features that make a good newspaper report.

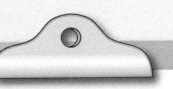

What have I learnt?

Read your newspaper report and check it contains the following features:

- a headline giving a summary of the story
- a headline using language features such as alliteration, rhyme, emotive words, rhetorical question
- the six paragraph plan from page 18, with paragraphs linked together appropriately
- emotive words used at key points in the report
- punctuation for effect
- synonyms – so that people's names are not repeated
- different sentence structures: simple, compound and complex
- commas – correctly used within sentences
- connectives – linking ideas together.

Unit 2 Biography, autobiography and diaries

Glossary

appendicitis: a serious illness in which the appendix becomes inflamed and painful

pneumonia: a lung infection

attaché: a person with a specialised area of responsibility

Roald Dahl (1916–1990), author of *Matilda, The BFG* and *Charlie and the Chocolate Factory*, is one of the most successful and beloved children's writers of all time. He ranks amongst the world's best-selling fiction authors with sales estimated at over 100 million, and his books have been published in almost 50 languages. Author J. K. Rowling named *Charlie and the Chocolate Factory* among her top ten books that every child should read.

Roald Dahl was born in Wales on 16th September 1916 to Norwegian parents. In 1920, when Dahl was three years old, his seven-year-old sister, Astri, died from **appendicitis**. Weeks later, his father died of **pneumonia** at the age of 57 while on a fishing trip in the Antarctic. At the age of eight, Dahl was sent off to a boarding school. His time there was fairly unhappy, providing some of the inspiration for his stories where the main characters are often neglected children and the villains adults who hate children.

At the outbreak of World War II, he signed up with the Royal Air Force as a fighter pilot. However, when he had to make a forced landing of his plane in the Libyan desert, he was severely injured, spending five months in a Royal Navy hospital in Alexandria, Egypt.

After his health returned, he was sent to Washington DC to work as an **attaché** – and this is where he started his writing career, when he was interviewed for an article in the *Saturday Evening Post* about his time as a fighter pilot. He offered to write about his experiences, and was immediately signed to write more articles.

In 1943 he wrote his first children's book, *The Gremlins*, but did not write another children's story until the 1960s. By this time he was a father himself and had started making up stories to entertain his own children. He went on to write 21 children's books including *The BFG, Matilda, The Witches* and *Charlie and the Chocolate Factory* – all of which have been made into films. Roald Dahl died on 23rd November 1990.

I understand the features of biographical and autobiographical texts.

Explore a biography

1 Read the extract from the biography of Roald Dahl on page 20.

  a Find and copy two quotations which show that Dahl had a successful career as a writer.

  b Write one word from paragraph 2 which means the same as *failing to care* or *look after someone properly*.

  c Dahl was a writer. What two other jobs did he have?

  d Write down the titles of four books written by Dahl.

  e Select the incident in Dahl's life which had an impact on what he wrote about in his children's books:

  * time at boarding school
  * experience as a journalist
  * his popularity
  * job as fighter pilot
  * flying accident in Libya
  * Norwegian parents
  * deaths of members of his family.

Helpful hints

A **biography** is a non-fiction text which recounts the story of someone's life. It usually starts when they were born, and goes through to the present date. If the person being written about is no longer alive, the biography ends with their death.

2 A biography concentrates on dates, ages and times. Using the extract on page 20, copy and complete the table below. Write what happened on the date or what the number indicates. The first one has been done for you.

1916	*This is when Roald Dahl was born.*
57	
five months	
eight	
1920	
1990	

Facts and opinions

1 The writer of the biography on page 20 has included both **facts** and **opinions**.
  a Find two facts.
  b Find two opinions.

2 Write two facts about your best friend and two opinions.

Some interesting facts about Roald Dahl
* He was 6 foot, 6 inches (1.98 metres).
* He nearly lost his nose in a car accident.
* He had nine children.
* He wrote his novels in his garden shed.
* He wrote the screen play for the James Bond film 'You only live twice' in 1967.
* He loved to eat chocolate, and admitted that he ate too much of it.

Did you know?

Helpful hints

* A **fact** is knowledge or information based on a real happening for which there is proof.
* An **opinion** is someone's view or belief, and not based on evidence. Clues to an opinion are words like *seems, may, might, should, could, just.* These words show the information is not exact. Adjectives such as *excellent, fantastic* will also indicate this is someone's opinion. Sometimes opinions pretend to be facts. For example, *estimate, millions, hundreds, crowds.* In the Roald Dahl biography on page 20 we have, ... *with sales estimated at over 100 million.*

Try this

Read the extract on page 20 again. Create a timeline which shows all the important events in Dahl's life.

Shades of meaning

I can explore shades of meaning in words.

Helpful hints

It is important to use words so that they convey exactly the right shade of meaning. For example, there is considerable difference between the words **big** and **huge**.

1 Rearrange the letters of these anagrams of words meaning 'big' and 'small'.

Big	Small
egarl	niyt
antgi	ltilte
guhe	emtiun
tavs	etpiet
menimse	icrscopoicm

2 Arrange the words from activity 1 in order of size.

Talk Partners

Share you answers with a talk partner. Did you agree? Why do you think it is difficult to get the order right?

Try this

Make a list of synonyms for 'good', 'beautiful' and 'nice'. When you are writing, try to use an exact word from these lists.

Features of biography

1 Here are some features of a biography. Copy and complete the table using examples from the biography of Roald Dahl on page 20.

Opening sums up why person should be remembered	*He ranks amongst the world's best-selling fiction authors.*
Dates in the order they happened	*Roald Dahl was born in Wales on 16th September 1916 … In 1920, when Dahl was three years old.*
Written in the third person	
Uses time connectives/phrases	
Focuses on significant events	*Death of father and sister.*
Ending highlights effect of person on the future	

2 Paragraphs are always about one particular topic. Write a sub-heading for each of the five paragraphs in the extract on page 20. For example, the first one could have the sub-heading, *Popular children's writer* or even just *Roald Dahl*.

The author's childhood experiences, the death of his sister and his father, the death of his own daughter and his unhappy years in boarding school, influenced his work as did his vivid imagination. Dahl's books might be called modern fairy tales. They are sometimes violent or horrific – but also humorous, and very entertaining! Children break free from their cruel adult oppressors and go on to have the most amazing adventures. Goodness always comes out tops, and evil is punished.

3 Read the extract opposite from the biography of Roald Dahl.

a Write another word or phrase which means the same as:
   vivid, influenced, oppressor.

b Why has the dash been used in sentence three? Select the correct answer to:
   - break up the sentence
   - signal something different
   - act as a pause
   - show surprise.

c What opposite themes could we expect to see in a children's book written by Roald Dahl?

I know how to write a biography and autobiography.

Writing biography and autobiography

1 You are going to write the first chapter of a biography of another learner in your class – stopping just before they first go to school. As it is the first chapter, you will need to find out things about their early life. You won't have time to write out their full answers, so make notes as shown below.

Jon Agu – 10 years old – born in Dubai in 2004 – now lives in Mumbai.

Ask the questions from the clipboard.

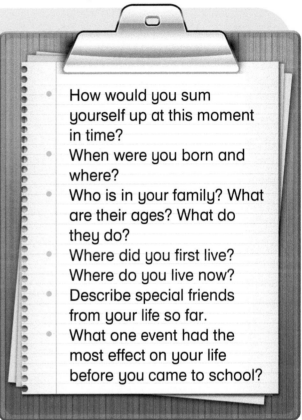

- How would you sum yourself up at this moment in time?
- When were you born and where?
- Who is in your family? What are their ages? What do they do?
- Where did you first live? Where do you live now?
- Describe special friends from your life so far.
- What one event had the most effect on your life before you came to school?

2 Write up the notes from activity 1 into four to five short paragraphs, and give each paragraph a title. The first paragraph should be a short summary of who you are writing about.

3 Ask the subject of the biography to read through what you have written, and suggest any improvements. Agree on one drawing that could be added. Your subject might agree to give you a photograph to use.

Writing presentation

Write up a final draft of your work. Remember to:

- Use the first paragraph as an introduction. For example, *Jahila Patel was born in 2004, and currently lives in Mumbai, India …*
- Write the events in time order.
- Add the photo or drawing.
- Divide the writing into paragraphs, linking paragraphs together appropriately.
- Include connectives to link events and ideas together.
- Conclude with the sentence, *So, it is now time for Jahila to attend her first school …*

Reading an autobiography

I can remember very little of the two years I spent at Llandaff Cathedral School, between the ages of seven and nine. Only two moments remain clearly in my mind. The first lasted not more than five seconds but I will never forget it.

It was my first term and I was walking home alone across the village green after school when suddenly one of the senior twelve-year-old boys came riding full speed down the road on his bicycle about twenty yards away from me. The road was on a hill and the boy was going down the slope, and as he flashed by he started backpedalling very quickly so that the free-wheeling mechanism of his bike made a loud whirring sound. At the same time, he took his hands off the handlebars and folded them casually across his chest. I stopped dead and stared after him. How wonderful he was! How swift and brave and graceful in his long trousers with bicycle clips around them and his scarlet school cap at a jaunty angle on his head! One day, I told myself, one glorious day I will have a bike like that and I will wear long trousers with bicycle-clips and my school cap will sit jaunty on my head and I will go whizzing down the hill pedalling backwards with no hands on the handlebars!

Boy: Tales of Childhood by Roald Dahl

I know the features of biography and autobiography texts and can compare them.

Comparing biography and autobiography

 Read the extract from Roald Dahl's autobiography, *Boy: Tales of Childhood* on page 26 and answer the questions.

a   Give six differences between Dahl's autobiography and the biography on page 20. The first one has been done for you.

Difference 1	*Autobiography written in the first person, biography in the third person*
Difference 2	
Difference 3	
Difference 4	
Difference 5	
Difference 6	

b   Which do you prefer – the biography or autobiography of Roald Dahl? Give a reason for your answer.

c   Find and write two adverbs in the extract which tell the reader how the boy was riding his bike.

d   Roald Dahl refers to the boy on the bike as 'swift and brave'. What does the boy do which shows this?

e   In the extract Roald Dahl has used grammar effectively to convey his feelings. Find one example each of:
- a simple sentence
- an exclamatory sentence
- a compound sentence
- repetition
- set of three adjectives
- powerful verbs.

Writing an autobiography

I know how to write an autobiography and what features to use.

1 What do you remember about your first day at school? If you can't remember, think about another significant event in your life instead. Copy and complete the spider diagram below to help you.

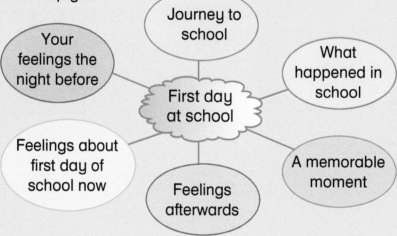

Journey to school

Your feelings the night before

What happened in school

First day at school

Feelings about first day of school now

Feelings afterwards

A memorable moment

2 Now write about your first day at school or another significant event. Organise your notes into paragraphs. Use adjectives to help the reader see what you saw:
The teacher gave a wide grin, her blue eyes seeming to glitter in the pale morning sun.

adjectives

Use **adverbs** so that the reader can experience what you felt:
Trembling **slightly**, I made my way into the classroom.

adverb

Start each paragraph like this:

- My first school was …
- The night before …
- The journey to school was …
- Once at school, …
- One memory which stands out is …
- My first school day had come to an end, and …
- Looking backing on my first day at school now, I think …

Prefixes and suffixes

1 'bio' is a Greek prefix meaning 'life'. Using a dictionary, find four other words which begin with 'bio' and write out the definitions.

2 'auto' is a Greek prefix meaning 'self'. Using a dictionary, find four other words which begin with 'auto', and write out the definitions.

3 'graph' is a Greek suffix meaning 'something written or drawn'. Use the clues below to give three other words which contain the suffix 'graph'.
  • A famous person's signature.
  • An image created by a camera.

4 Change the words in the cloud below by adding on one of the following prefixes, all of which mean 'not':

un   il   ir   im   dis

repair   loyal   natural   comfort   regular   moral   happy   usual
legal   rational   mobile   necessary   logical   responsible   possible

5 The prefix 'ab' means 'away, from'. Using a dictionary, find three words beginning with this prefix, and write out the meanings.

6 The prefix 'ad' means 'to, toward'. Using a dictionary, find three words beginning with ad. Write down the meanings.

Word origins and derivations

1 Copy and complete this table. Add two other words to word root families. The first one has been done for you.

Root Family	Word 1	Word 2
aquatic	*aquarius*	*aquarium*
auditorium		
circuit		
dentist		
equal		
magnify		
minimum		
zoo		

Helpful hints

Many English words are based on Greek or Latin roots. For example, the root word 'scribe' meaning to write, has led to words such as manuscript, scripture, and postscript.

2 Work out what these word roots mean.

a aqua **b** audio **c** circ **d** dent **e** equ **f** magn **g** min **h** zoo

Use an online etymological dictionary to check whether you were correct.

3 **a** Sort the words below containing word roots into four columns. Then write the word root at the top of each column. (Hint. One root is 'auto'.)

autograph   telephone   biceps   automatic   transatlantic   bisect
telegraph   transfer   automaton   telescope   bicycle   transport   bifocals
autobiography   television   bilingual   transparent   autopsy   telepathy
automobile   translate   telephoto   biannual   transplant

4 Below are words borrowed from other countries:

dollar   marmalade   trek   barbecue   bungalow   shampoo

a Guess which of the following countries these words were originally from:
Portugal   Germany   Caribbean   India   South Africa
Write out each country, and then write the words next to it.

b Now use the internet or a dictionary to see if you were right.

I can change the meanings of words by adding suffixes.

Suffixes

1 Change the meaning of these words by adding a suffix from the list below. Check with a partner to see if you agree. You may need to consult a dictionary.

ship	hood	ness	ment

a member	b child	c fair	d enjoy	e owner
f false	g kind	h fellow	i employ	j partner
k father	l manage	m mother	n wicked	o fit

2 Use each word from activity 1 to write a sentence of your own.

3 One of the functions of a suffix is to change the word class. It can change an adjective into a noun, a verb into a noun, a noun to a verb. Which class have the words below been changed to? The first two have been done for you.

a hard – hardness (adjective into a noun)
b educate – education (verb into a noun)
c simple – simplicity
d able – ability
e deepen – deep
f create – creation
g happy – happiness
h length – lengthen

4 Copy and complete the table below. Give a synonym and antonym for the word, keeping the word class the same.

Word	Synonym	Antonym
hide	*conceal*	*show*
happiness		
quietly		
angry		

Diaries

Samuel Pepys started his diary in 1660. He went on writing it until 1669. It's full of information, because Pepys was interested in everything around him. In this diary extract, he writes about the Great Fire of London. Some of the words and expression are different because the diary was written a long time ago.

Diary extract 1:

2nd September 1666

About seven rose again to dress myself, and there looked out at the window, and saw the fire not so much as it was and further off. So to my **closet** to set things to rights after yesterday's cleaning. By and by Jane comes and tells me that she hears that above 300 houses have been burned down to-night by the fire we saw last night, and that it is now burning down all Fish-street, by London Bridge. So I made myself ready presently, and walked to the Tower, and there got up upon one of the high places, Sir J. Robinson's little son going up with me; and there I did see the houses at that end of the bridge all on fire, and an **infinite** great fire on this and the other side the end of the bridge. So down, with my heart full of trouble, to the Lieutenant of the Tower, who tells me that it begun this morning in the King's baker's house in Pudding lane. And that it hath burned St. Magnus's Church and most part of Fish-street already. So I down to the water-side, and there got a boat and through bridge, and there saw a **lamentable** fire. Poor Michell's house, as far as the Old Swan, already burned that way, and the fire running further, that in a very little time it got as far as the Steeleyard, while I was there. Everybody **endeavouring** to remove their goods, and flinging into the river; poor people staying in their houses as long as till the very fire touched them, and then running into boats, or **clambering** from one pair of stairs by the water-side to another.

Glossary

closet: small private room
infinite: without end
lamentable: terrible
endeavouring: trying
clambering: climbing awkwardly

Here is another diary extract. It is written by a writer pretending to be someone who lived nearly 150 years ago. They had to stay in a workhouse – a place where poor people went to live and work.

Diary extract 2:

4th January 1871

Stoneleigh Workhouse is a dreadful place. From the outside it is a grim-looking building with rows of uncurtained windows, and the way in is through a large oak door that creaks and groans like a **banshee** *when it swings open on its huge hinges. My spirits* **plummeted** *further the moment I stepped inside. It was bleak in the extreme and the occasional hissing gaslights did little to* **dispel** *the gloom. High, echoing corridors, dark-green paint and not a single ornament or decoration to lighten the depressing effect. It is January but there seemed to be little in the way of heating, though somewhere there must have been a fire because ghostly wisps of bitter-smelling smoke drifted in the cold air of the gloomy corridor.*

We waited for the meeting in a dingy office full of files and ledgers. There was a rug on the floor and a comfortable chair for the workhouse Master. His name is Alfred Frumley and I took against him instantly. He is big and burly with a flat nose and dark, **gimlet** *eyes. His mouth has a cruel twist to it and he gives the impression that he doesn't know what love means. Why, I wondered, was he appointed to such a position? Does he rule with an iron will?*

This diary extract is taken from My Story: Workhouse by Pamela Oldfield.

Glossary

banshee: wailing woman
plummeted: sank
dispel: remove
gimlet: small and sharp

This third diary extract comes from the series, *Diary of a Wimpy Kid* written by Jeff Kinney, and is about a boy living in the 21st century.

Diary extract 3:   Saturday September 10th

Well, this first week of school finally over so I can sleep late. Most kids set their alarms and get up early on a Saturday morning to watch cartoons or whatever, but not me.

Unfortunately, Dad wakes up at 6am in the morning no matter what day it is, and he is not really considerate of the fact that I'm trying to enjoy my Saturday. Often, he will set to vacuuming the whole house, including my bedroom!

While I'm on the subject of Saturday, I should mention some of my gripes. First of all there's nothing on TV after 1.00pm except golf and bowling.

Second of all, the sun comes through the window and you can hardly see what's on the TV anyway. And on top of that you get sweaty and stick to the couch. It's a conspiracy against kids to make them go outside and do something else besides watch TV.

1 Read the three diary extracts on pages 32–34. Answer these questions.

a Give three main differences between diaries 1, 2 and 3. Write your answer out like this: Diary extract 1 was written a long time ago. It tells you where the event happened and an outline of what happened, but there is little description. Diary extract 2 ...; Diary extract 3 ...

b Copy and complete the table below. Answer by writing in: Y (yes); N (no); NS (not sure)

Glossary

gripes: complaints
conspiracy: a secret plan by adults

Language Features Diary			
Diary:	Pepys	Workhouse	Wimpy Kid
Written in the first person			
Mentions times/dates			
Events told in chronological order			
Gives feelings			
Gives description			
Gives detail of places			
Mostly in the past tense			
Uses chatty or informal style			

c Which diary extract style do you prefer? Why?

Write a diary

I know what language features to use when writing a diary.

a Keep a diary entry over one day.
- Write in the first person.
- Recount events in chronological order. Start in the morning and end when you go to bed.
- Start a new paragraph when you shift topic, or if there is a major shift in time. For example, going from the morning to the afternoon.
- On some events, include your feelings and comments. 'After PE, I felt so exhausted …'.
- Imagine someone is going to read your diary. Build in some descriptive detail to help them see people or things, 'Heavy rain battered the school window'.
- Adopt a chatty, informal style – as if you are actually speaking to friend.

b What are the benefits of keeping a diary? Would you like to carry on writing one?

Writing presentation

Write a diary entry from the point of view of a well-known fairy story character. For example, the Prince or one of the ugly sisters in 'Cinderella'.
Use the following sentence starters to help you write your diary.

- *The morning started off well …*
- *After that, it was …*
- *Just when I was thinking that I couldn't face any more …*
- *You wouldn't believe it, but then …*
- *Thoroughly exhausted …*

What have I learnt?

Read your diary entry and check it has the following features. My diary:
- is written in the first person
- has the day and date written at the top of each diary entry
- has events recounted in order of time, using connectives where possible
- has a new paragraph when there is a shift of topic, or a big shift in time
- makes comments on feelings, using punctuation such as an exclamation mark
- makes some description visual so that a reader can see what I have written about
- uses the correct spelling, punctuation and grammar.

Unit 3 Reports and argument

Non-chronological report linked to work in other subjects

1 Read through these notes on the bottlenose dolphin.

Bottlenose Dolphin
- Short stubby beak (hence name 'bottlenose')
- Typically measures 2–4 m; weighs 135–650 kg. Males much bigger than females.
- Skin grey, smooth; flakes off so replaced every few hours.
- 18–26 pairs of sharp teeth on each side of jaw, but usually swallow their prey whole.
- Consumes 8–15 kg (15–30 lbs) food per day.
- Swim speeds up to 35 km/h; dives as deep as 915 m.
- Take turns herding fish into smaller areas for others to eat.
- Get food by knocking fish out of the water with tails, then eats them.
- Swim in groups (called pods) of 10–25, but are found in larger herds of several hundred.
- Listen for echo of sound then work out shape/location of their prey (echolocation).
- Surf on waves; create bubble rings with their blowholes.
- Communicate through squeaks/whistles; leaping from water and slapping their tails.
- Can hold breath for up to seven minutes, but must come to surface to breathe air.
- Never fully sleep – one side of their brain must always be active so they remember to breathe.

Helpful hints

A **non-chronological report** contains information but this is not organised in order of time, as in a story. For example, if the report is about an animal, it might begin by reporting what it looks like, then move onto where it lives, how it moves and rears its young – finishing with any particular habits.

2

a Using the notes above, write a non-chronological report on the bottlenose dolphin. You will need to:
- Sort the information into four or five areas. For example, appearance, eating habits, movement and interesting facts.
- Decide on the order of your areas. Which one will come first or last?
- Think about how to link and expand the notes. For example, '*The bottle nose dolphin …, It …, They …, As a species …, Together …, As a group …, An interesting fact is that …, Believe it or not …*'.

b Once you have completed the report, add an illustration that would be helpful to a reader – such as a labelled drawing of the bottlenose dolphin.

Active and passive verbs

Helpful hints

Verbs can be **active** or **passive**. All passive verbs are made up of the verb to **be** + **past participle (ing/ ed/ irregular ending)**:

- *We **are hoping** you will be seen (by them).*
- *The glass **has been broken** (by her).*
- *It was **discovered** (by him).*

In the **active** voice, the subject is the 'agent' (the doer) of the action expressed in the verb. The object of the sentence is the receiver of the action.

- **Ben** delivered the **parcel**.

  (doer) Active

In the **passive** voice, the sentence is flipped so that the object becomes the subject. This means the subject is now the receiver of the action instead of the 'agent' (the doer).

- The parcel **was delivered** by Ben.

  (receiver) Passive

Passive sentences which withhold or conceal the agent (the doer) are useful when you just want to report something that has happened – and not anything else.

- *This vase has been broken.*

---

1 Change the following sentences into the passive voice:

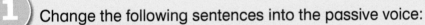

- a The man decorated the house.
- b The pirate hid the treasure under the tree.
- c The children sang a song at the start of the concert.
- d The ambulance took the man to hospital.
- e The gardener grew beautiful flowers.

2 Find another five examples of sentences where the verb is in the passive voice. You may find them in other text books – especially those reporting information.

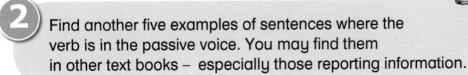

Report of a controversial issue

I know how controversial arguments can be presented effectively.

Helpful hints

In report writing, information should be presented in an impersonal way without any personal comment. This can be difficult when the writer has strong feelings!

1 Read this report on a controversial issue.
The writer has not written it in an impersonal way.

My name is Jonas Hernez. I have lived in this town all my life and am absolutely furious about the plan to build a new road to run right through the middle of it. **I think it will result in many houses and shops being ruined.** It is a disgrace. Our town will end up being like every other town, full of traffic and noise. **I think the result will be a significant increase in pollution levels.**

There is also the cost. I have heard millions and millions are going to be spent. That is disgraceful! Surely we could find better things to do with such a large sum of money?
For example, build a local swimming pool and sports centre for our young people; create a park for the older generation; establish new businesses **so we can provide jobs.** If we were given the money, we could make a real difference to the people who live in our community.

Writing a report

1 Re-write the report on page 38 so that is impersonal. It should have no reference to the speaker, no personal comments or feelings expressed. In order to make the report impersonal and balanced, you will need to:
- Take out all the references to the writer and emotive statements.
- Take out /change the personal pronouns.
- Change some of the sentences from the active voice to the passive voice. These have been underlined in the report.

> For example:
> **Active:** *I think it will result in many houses and shops being ruined.*
> Will change to
>
>
>
> **Passive**: *The result will be the ruin of many houses and shops.*

Your new version should start like this:
The building of a new road has been proposed. The plans state that ...

2 When you have finished activity 1, read the two versions of the report aloud.

a   The first one, on page 38 (which includes personal feelings) should put emphasis on language which is more emotive, such as 'absolutely furious'. What other words and phrases would you emphasise?

b   The second re-written version (which contains no personal feelings) should be read out in a much more matter-of-fact tone. Remember to enunciate all the vowels and consonants so that each word can be heard clearly.

Think about something you feel strongly about. This could be to do with school or where you live. Write one paragraph where you show your emotions and then another where there is no emotion shown. Which paragraph did you prefer?

Try this

Reports which influence the reader

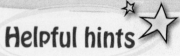

Helpful hints

Often reports are written with the intention of influencing the reader's opinion. The writer wants the reader to agree with them!

3.5 million sharks killed every year just for soup!

Staff from London's Sea Life London Aquarium joined forces with the charity Bite Back to stage a march in London's Chinatown to highlight the fight against shark fin soup.

The object of the march was to urge members to avoid shark fin soup during the Chinese New Year celebrations. Shark fin soup is considered a delicacy in some cultures and is still sold in many restaurants around the world despite its negative impact on the shark population. Many people consider it to have health benefits.

Around 3.5 million sharks are killed each year just for their fins, while the rest of their body is thrown away. In large parts of the oceans, the population of sharks is already down by 90 per cent or more in just the last 20 years. This problem is made worse because sharks reproduce very slowly, taking years to reach maturity and producing very few young sharks.

Some people think that killing sharks is no different to killing cows and sheep for food. However, sharks have survived for 450 million years and we are on course for killing off the whole species within a few years.

1 Read the report on shark fin soup and answer these questions.
  a List all the negative words and phrases from the article which highlight how unacceptable shark fin soup is. For example, 'the rest of their body is thrown away'.
  b List all the positive words and phrases about shark fin soup.
  c What is your view on shark fin soup? Give three reasons for your opinion.

Consonant choices

1 Sort the following words into three columns as shown in the table below. Those words that use '**k**' at the **beginning** of the word, those that use it in the **middle** and those that use it at the **end**.

k at the beginning	*k* in the middle	*k* at the end
keen	*tickle*	*back*

keep   tickle   kick   kept   back   pickle   keen   work   choking
kettle   tank   sink   crackle   wink
kit   stricken   walk   king   talk   wrinkle
ache   milk   kitten   ankle   smack

2 Copy and complete this table. Sort these words using **ci**, **ce** and **cy** into three columns. The first one has been done for you.

ci	ce	cy
cinema	*cereal*	*fancy*

fancy	circle	celebrate	accident	incident
cereal	circuit	recent	decide	discipline
centre	certificate	circus	decision	mercy
cyclist	cylinder	citizen	cellar	recite
cinema	circular	lacy	centigrade	certain
receive	decent	city	cyclone	ceremony
cinnamon	cynical	cynic	deceit	cyst
ceiling	circulation	celebrity	century	
Cypress	cement	bicycle	decimal	

3 Read the words from activity 1 and 2 aloud. From this list choose six words that are new to you, look up their meaning in a dictionary and use them in a sentence of your own.

Investigate the use of a conditional sentence

I know how to write a conditional sentence.

Helpful hints

A **conditional sentence** is where one thing depends on another.

- *If you don't get up now, you will be late for school.*
- *Let us go swimming on Friday, **unless it's raining**.*

1 Complete the following conditional sentences
   a   If I keep fit, I will be able to ...
   b   If I help at home, I might be able to ...
   c   If I work hard, I should be able to ...
   d   If I go home this way, I may ...
   e   I will come and visit you this evening , unless ...

2 Imagine you have unexpectedly won a lot of money.
Complete the following sentences:
   a   If I win a lot of money, I will ...
   b   If I win a lot of money, I might ...
   c   If I win a lot of money, I could ...
   d   If I win a lot of money, I should ...
   e   If I win a lot of money, I must ...
   f   If I win a lot of money, I may ...

Writing presentation

Write a paragraph explaining what you would like to do when you grow up, and how you can prepare for this now. Use as many different types of conditional sentences as you can. For example:
When I grow up, I would like to be doctor. However, I can only do this if I work hard ...

Features of written arguments

An argument

A learner has been asked to put forward an argument on why there should be more time in school spent on sport and physical exercise. This is presented as a speech to the class.

Good morning, everyone.
My name is Maria Anjou, and I am here today to present my argument on whether there should be more time in school spent on sport and physical exercise. Presently, we only have one hour a week. I strongly believe we should have more time, and here are my reasons why.

Firstly, research has shown that sport and exercise are very important in keeping children healthy. If children do too little exercise, they are much more likely to sit around watching television, playing on their computer and eating junk food. This can cause them to lack energy and put on weight. If we had one hour of exercise every day instead of once a week, think what a difference this would make!

Secondly, a regular exercise slot every day at school would help children get into the habit of continuing some form of exercise at home. If this happened, they would be less likely to play on computers and watch television all day eating junk food.

Thirdly, exercise and sport helps you learn. Scientists say that even 30 minutes of exercise a day is enough to have a positive effect. Exercise pumps more blood to your brain, making it more alert. More oxygen means healthier brain cells. There is no doubt that regular exercise makes you smarter.

To conclude, one hour of sport and exercise a week is simply not enough. More time is needed because this will make the children of our school healthier and more effective as learners. Which school would not want that?

Helpful hints

Arguments attempt to win the reader over to the writer's point of view. Good arguments will present reasons based largely on facts, rather than opinions. The argument is stated at the beginning so that the reader knows what to expect. It then builds up, point by point, towards a conclusion where the argument is then repeated, so it is the last point the reader is left with!

Argument texts

I know the features of argument texts.

Helpful hints

A **set of three** can be three words, three phrases or three sentences in a row, used to create effect.

1 Read the argument text on page 43 and answer these questions.

  a Sum up the writer's three main arguments as to why there should be more sport in school.

  b Find and write an example of three connectives used in the argument. These can be words or phrases.

  c The writer provides facts to support her argument. Find and write two examples of facts.

  d A number of language features have been used to make the argument seem convincing and persuasive. Copy this table and write in examples.

Feature	Example
A set of three	
Rhetorical question	
Short sentence for effect	
Adverb used for emphasis	
Exaggerated opinion	
Use of conditional sentence to present an argument	
Confident phrases	

2 Which language feature from the table is:

  a new to you?

  b did you already know about?

I can argue a case in writing and develop my points logically.

Presenting an argument

 1 Prepare a speech arguing **for** *or* **against** one of the following:

- Should computers replace teachers?
- Should children be allowed to bring mobile phones to school?
- Should the school day be two hours shorter?

You may feel that there are arguments on both sides, but for this activity you must simply either argue **for** *or* **against**.

Use the table below to structure your speech. It gives you a plan for each paragraph and tells you what language features to include.

Paragraph 1	Introduce yourself. State the argument. Give your view.
Paragraph 2	State your first point in favour of your paragraph. Use the rest of the paragraph to prove it, by using: <ul><li>examples and facts</li><li>assertive opinions</li><li>rhetorical devices, e.g. sets of three, rhetorical question, adverbs for emphasis, short sentence for effect.</li></ul>
Paragraph 3	Use the same formula as for paragraph 2, but with another main point.
Paragraph 4	Use the same formula as for paragraph 2, but with another main point.
Paragraph 5	This is the final paragraph. Restate your argument, and give the most important reason for it. Finish with a rhetorical question.

Talk Partners

Present your argument to a partner or the class using your notes from activity 1. Remember to follow the paragraph plan and to use the language features suggested:

- include examples and facts
- assert your opinions. For example, *There is no doubt that ...*
- use sets of three. For example, *no time to play, socialise or relax*
- use adverbs for emphasis. For example, *passionately believe*
- use short sentence for emphasis. For example, *Mobile phones are essential.*

A balanced argument

1 A balanced argument is where you should consider both sides of the argument. Make a balanced argument about one of these topics.

- Should school uniform be compulsory?
- Should learners be allowed to bring pets to school?
- Should parents be able to observe lessons?

A balanced argument needs a different kind of planning to a **for** or **against** argument. Look at how it has been done in the table below.

The argument: Should the school cafeteria offer fast food rather than school lunches?	
Arguments for	**Arguments against**
Will be more popular with children.	More unhealthy.
Can be served quicker, so giving children more time to play or relax.	Will encourage children to rush food.
Cheaper than a school lunch.	Children might buy more lunch so it could end up being more expensive.

Copy the table above to make notes on the argument you have chosen to write about. Remember to have opposite points on each of the three rows. Ask a partner whether they find these points clear.

Writing an argument

These example paragraphs will help you write your balanced argument.

The first paragraph will let the reader know that you have arguments for *and* against the topic.

> *Should the school cafeteria offer fast food rather than school lunches? My opinion is that there are arguments both for and against, and here are my reasons why.*

The next paragraph will have to balance the both for and against argument. For example:

> *Firstly, there is no doubt that many children would prefer fast food at lunch time such as chips or pizza. It is good to have something different to what we get served at home, and it makes lunch more cool and exciting. However, although fast food may be preferred by learners, it is not always healthy. It often contains too much sugar, fat and additives. Research shows us that if children eat junk food, it can make them restless, and unable to concentrate. We don't want that, do we as we go into afternoon lessons?*

Even though the writer has presented both sides of the argument, it can be seen that they are a little more against the idea than for it.

The final paragraph will need to tell the reader which side you come down on.

> *The arguments presented show that the option to have fast foods rather than school lunch is not a straightforward one. Although it might be popular with learners, it would not be healthy, and that is why I am against it.*

Writing presentation

Use your plan from page 46 and the example paragraphs above to help you write a balanced argument on your chosen topic. The argument should be four to five paragraphs long and the paragraphs should link together appropriately so that your argument is clear to the reader. The first paragraph must introduce the argument, and the final one give your point of view.

Talk Partners

In pairs, read aloud and listen to each other's balanced arguments. Discuss which argument appears to be the most effective, and the reasons for this.

Fiction

Read the extract and answer ALL the questions which follow.

Extract from *Tom's Midnight Garden*

Tom has been sent to stay with his uncle and aunt while his brother Peter recovers from measles.

His uncle pulled up outside a pillared front door, and Aunt Gwen appeared in the doorway, laughing and wanting to kiss Tom. She drew him inside and Uncle Alan followed with the luggage. There were cold stone flags under Tom's feet, and in his nostrils a smell of old dust that it had been nobody's business to disperse. As he looked around he felt a chill. The hall of the house was not mean nor was it ugly, but it was unwelcoming. Someone had pinned bright travel posters to the high grey walls. Someone had left a laundry box with its laundry list, in a corner. There were empty milk bottles against a far door with a message for the milkman. None of these things seemed to really belong to the hall. It remained empty and silent – silent that is except for the voice of Aunt Gwen chattering on about Tom's mother and Peter's measles. When her voice died for a moment, Tom heard the only sound that went on: the tick, then the tick, and then tick, and then tick of a grandfather clock.

'No, don't touch, Tom,' said Aunt Gwen. She lowered her voice, 'It belongs to old Mrs. Bartholomew upstairs, and she's rather particular about it.'

Tom had never looked inside a grandfather clock before, and he thought it might be something he could do later, privately. Surely he could just look quickly, now. With his back to the clock, innocently continuing to converse with his aunt, he slipped his finger nails under the edge of the pendulum door …

'If Mrs. Bartholomew is so particular about her clock, why doesn't she have it upstairs with her?' Tom asked. He levered gently with his fingernails: the door was resisting him.

'Because the clock is screwed to the wall at the back and the screws have rusted in,' said Aunt Gwen. 'Come away from it, Tom. Come up to tea.'

'Oh,' Tom said, as if he had not realised where he was standing.

As they made their way upstairs to the Kitson's flat, from behind them, the grandfather clock struck one with steely emphasis, although its fingers pointed to 5 o' clock …

Tom's Midnight Garden by Philippa Pearce

1   Give one piece of evidence from the text which shows that the house
    is made up of flats.   (1)

2   Which four items are in the hall of the house?   (2)

3   Give a quotation which suggests no one looked after the hall.   (1)

4   How does the reader know the grandfather clock has been there
    a long time?   (1)

5   Why does the writer say of Aunt Gwen, 'She lowered her voice.'?   (1)

6   What makes Tom stop trying to open the grandfather clock?   (1)

7   Find evidence from the text that shows Tom is secretive.   (1)

8   'As they made their way upstairs to the Kitson's flat, from behind
    them, the grandfather clock struck one with <u>steely</u> <u>emphasis</u>, although
    its fingers pointed to 5 o' clock …' Replace the two words underlined with
    another word or phrase which means the same.   (2)

9   Give two adjectives which show the house was not welcoming.   (2)

10 Why has the writer repeated 'Someone' at the beginning of two sentences? (1)

11 'With his back to the clock, innocently continuing to converse with his
    aunt, he slipped his finger nails under the edge of the pendulum door … '
    a   Identify the prepositional phrase and explain why it has been
        placed at the beginning of the sentence.   (2)
    b   Give one adverb which shows that Tom
        was careful in what he did.   (1)

12 Choose the genre of the extract.
    a   Real life story
    b   Horror
    c   Fantasy
    d   Diary
    e   Myth   (1)

13 Whose point of view does the story
    focus on, and how do we know?   (2)

14 Explain why an ellipsis has been used
    at the end of the extract.   (1)

PRACTICE TEST 1

Non-fiction

Read the extract and answer ALL the questions which follow.

Clock towers

A clock tower is a tower which has been built so as to have one or more (often four) clock faces. Clock towers can be either freestanding or part of a church or a building such as a town hall. The mechanism inside the tower is known as a turret clock; this often marks the hour (and sometimes segments of an hour) by sounding large bells or chimes.

Elizabeth Tower

Before the middle of the twentieth century, most people did not have watches, and prior to the 18th century even home clocks were rare. The first clocks did not have faces, as these were only on striking clocks, which sounded bells to call the surrounding community to work or to prayer. These clocks were placed in towers so the bells would be audible from a long distance. Clock towers were placed near the centres of towns and would be very tall. As clock towers became more common, the designers realised that a dial on the outside of the tower would allow the townspeople to read the time whenever they wanted.

Rajabai Tower

Clock towers are a common sight in many parts of the world with some being famously known landmarks. Three of the best-known are Elizabeth Tower built in 1859, which houses the Great Bell (generally known as *Big Ben*) in London; the Rajabai Tower in Mumbai and the Royal Mecca Clock Tower in Saudi Arabia – which is the largest clock tower in the world. It is also the tallest building in Saudi Arabia, with a height of 601 metres, and is the third tallest freestanding structure in the world.

Royal Mecca Clock Tower

1   How does the mechanism inside a clock tower work?   (1)

2   How frequently did early clock towers let people know the time?   (1)

3   Give three visual features of clock towers that would help people know the time. (2)

4   Why would clock towers be referred to as landmarks?   (1)

5   Explain why the text finishes with a reference to the Royal Mecca Clock Tower?   (1)

6   Put the following words or phrases from the text into your own words:
    a   'prior'
    b   'surrounding community'
    c   'common sight'
    d   'freestanding structure'.   (4)

7   Suggest a subheading for paragraphs 1, 2 and 3.   (3)

8   'Royal Mecca Clock Tower in Saudi Arabia – which is the largest clock tower
    in the world.' Why has a dash been used in this sentence?   (1)

9   'And this often marks the hour (and sometimes segments of an hour)
    by sounding large bells or chimes.' Why have brackets been used in
    this sentence?   (1)

10 The text uses largely facts. Give one example of a fact from the text.   (1)

11 Rewrite the second paragraph to include the main points in no more
    than 40 words.   (4)

12 From the text, find an example of a:
    a   verb phrase
    b   pronoun
    c   proper noun
    d   comparative adjective.   (4)

13 Copy this sentence then underline the
    main clause.

    They were placed in towers so the bells
    would be audible from a long distance.   (1)

14 From paragraph 1, find and write an
    example of a compound sentence.   (1)

15 Copy and correct the errors in this sentence:
    Bells in clocks is crucial so the people
    can hear clearly.   (2)

Big Ben's bell

16 Rewrite this sentence adding the two missing apostrophes:
    Clocks arent used by everyone today but its still important to have
    them as historic landmarks.   (2)

Non-fiction: reading and writing skills

Explicit and implicit meaning

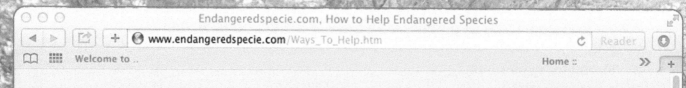

Endangeredspecie.com, How to Help Endangered Species

www.endangeredspecie.com/Ways_To_Help.htm   Reader

Welcome to ..   Home ::

Endangered species need your help!

Here are some ways that you can become involved

- One of the best ways to help threatened plants and animals is to protect their **habitats** in national parks, nature reserves and other wildlife areas where they might live, such as farms and along roadsides. These are places which should have little or no interference from humans.

- When you visit a national park or reserve, make sure you obey the wildlife code: follow fire regulations; leave any pets at home; do not touch or remove any animals or plants (including trees); put your rubbish in a bin; do not make unnecessary noise – and behave respectably.

- If you have friends who live on a farm, encourage them to ask their parents (if possible) to protect old trees. These often have hollows which are good for nesting animals, and – into the bargain – provide valuable shade.

Glossary

habitat: where an animal lives

Did you know?

There are currently over 3,000 animals listed as endangered, compared to 1,000 animals listed in 1998.

I can find explicit and implicit information in a text.

Helpful hints

- Some questions about texts require you to find **explicit** information. This is information which is clearly stated in the text, and not 'hidden' in any way. Usually, all you have to do is to find it!
- **Implicit** meaning is when you have to work out what the writer might be suggesting or implying – a bit like a detective working from clues. For example, if there is a wet pair of shoes mentioned in a text, it could be inferred that it's been raining! With implicit questions you often have to show how you worked out the answer.

1 Read the extract on page 52 from a website about how children can help endangered species. Answer these **explicit** questions.

DRIVE WITH CAUTION YOU ARE ENTERING AN ENDANGERED SPECIES AREA

   a   Give four areas where threatened plants and animals live.

   b   How many regulations are there in the wildlife code?

   c   Find and write two pieces of evidence from the text which shows keeping old trees is good for wildlife.

2 Now answer these **implicit** questions about the website information on page 52.

   a   Read through the wildlife code regulations. Which two regulations seem to be saying almost the same thing? Explain the reason for your answer.

   b   Write a word or phrase from the website which shows that plants and wildlife are not yet free from human interference.

   c   What might be the issue with asking 'friends who live on a farm' to keep old trees for wildlife to live in?

Talk Partners

Compare your answers with a talk partner.
Do you have the same explanations for questions 2a–c?

I understand the colon and know when to use it.

Colons

1 Which examples use the capital letter correctly after the colon?

a I am very interested in many different sorts of sports: Football, rugby, tennis, running and athletics.

b The following learners have been chosen for the school football team: Jamil Abadan, Jonas Alsam, Lucy Casteraz, Natalie Smith.

c For my birthday, I received so many presents. These included some expensive items: a new tennis racquet; a ticket to the new theme park; a large box of sweets and a new pair of trainers.

Helpful hints

A **colon** is a punctuation mark which consists of two dots – one on top of the other. It looks like this :

One way the colon can be used is to show that a list is going to follow.

* *When you visit a national park or reserve, make sure you obey the wildlife code :*
  follow fire regulations …
  leave any pets at home …
* *For school tomorrow I need :*
  a swimming bag, my lunch money and history text book.

A colon is not as strong as a full stop. The first letter of the word after the colon should have a lower case letter – unless it is a proper noun.

d Please bring the following with you when we go out on Sunday: A map, some sandwiches, a rope and a pair of sunglasses.

2 Re-write these sentences, adding a colon and then a list of items. Remember to use capital letters correctly.

a This is what is in my bedroom.

b Here is a list of what makes me feel happy.

c This equipment is needed to play football.

d The following learners are going on the school trip.

Try this

Make up six sentences of your own that use a colon correctly. Ask a partner to mark these. Did you get them all correct? Aim to use colons in your own writing when a list has to be introduced.

More about colons

Helpful hints

Does a colon always come before a list? No!
The clause that comes before the colon should make sense on its own.

✓ *The boy's school bag contained some interesting items : one trainer;
a mouldy sandwich; last year's report card and a small stone.*

> A colon can be used with this clause. It makes sense on its own.

✗ *The boy's schoolbag contained one trainer, a mouldy sandwich,
last year's report card and an old scarf.*

> A colon cannot be used with this clause. It does not make sense on its own.

1 Which of these sentences has used the colon correctly to introduce a list?
Check the clause carefully!

a   You will need to: bring three things to the party, some crisps,
a few sandwiches and a large smile!

b   I was hoping to: tell all my class mates about the countries I visited,
the different people and the range of food I ate while on holiday.

c   Here are some important tips for doing well at school: work hard,
be respectful, like learning and always do your homework.

2 Write these introductory clauses so that they make
sense on their own and then add a colon and a list.

a   I need to
b   These learners are
c   The shop is
d   The wardrobe was

3 Write three sentences of your own which correctly use
an introductory clause and a colon before a list.

Using colons

Helpful hints

The colon can also be used to show something suggested in the first clause is going to be explained.
For example:
* *I will tell you what I'm going to do: I'm going to visit Africa.*
* *This is why I dislike rice pudding: it is too creamy and squishy.*

1 Expand these clauses by adding a colon then a second clause which either gives an explanation or an example. The first one has been done for you.

a   I will explain why I am cross: you did not turn up on time.
b   I hope you like this.
c   This is why I do not want to come.

2 Write three introductory clauses of your own, and then:
* Place the colon at the end of the clause.
* Add an explanation, for example, which explains or expands on the first clause.
Use the examples from question 1 to help you with this activity.

Writing presentation

Create a poster on the colon which would help a younger class to understand what it is, and how it should be used to introduce a list. Remember to include:
* what it looks like
* when a capital letter should be used
* how the introductory clause needs to make sense on its own.
Give examples to help make each point clear.

Semi-colons

I understand the semi-colon and when to use it.

Helpful hints

A **semi-colon** is a punctuation mark with a comma and a full stop on top above it. It looks like this ;
A semi-colon can be used to separate phrases in a list. For example:

When you visit a national park or reserve, make sure you obey the wildlife code: follow fire regulations; leave any pets at home; do not touch or remove any animals or plants (including trees); put your rubbish in a bin; do not make unnecessary noise – behave respectably.

As a general rule, the phrases separated by a semi-colon should be at least three words long. Otherwise, commas should be used.

1 Re-write these sentences, inserting semi-colons to separate phrases in the list.

a I need to buy the following for tonight's meal: one kilo of sausages one large bag of white flour five large onions and some bananas for dessert.

b The list of items needed for school are as follows: an electronic calculator a protractor for mathematics a good pocket dictionary a blue and a black pen for English a large file to keep work in.

c These items were packed in my suitcase a coat in case of rain two pairs of trousers two new T-shirts three woollen jumpers one additional pair of shoes and my favourite red dress.

2 Write three sentences which use a colon to introduce a list, and semi-colons to separate phrases in a list. These sentences should be about:

- What you intend doing next weekend.
- What you would like for your birthday.
- How to make your favourite meal.

Try this

Make up six sentences of your own that use semi-colons and a colon correctly. Ask a partner to mark these. Did you get them all correct? Aim to use semi-colons in your own writing to separate phrases of more than three words long when they are in a list.

Semi-colons and clauses

Helpful hints

Another way to use a semi-colon is to join together two related clauses into one sentence. Here, the semi-colon takes the place of **and**, **so** or **but**. For example:

- *The boy came into the class; he looked at me.* (semi-colon used instead of **and**).
- *I like cheese; my friend hates it.* (semi-colon used instead of **but**).

These sentences could exist as separate sentences, or even be joined together by **and** or **but**. However, the semi-colon is more subtle. It requires the reader to work out the relationship between the two sentences. Whether a writer uses a semi-colon or not will be a matter of choice. For example:

- *The teacher marched forward. He pointed at me.*
- *The teacher marched forward and pointed at me.*
- *The teacher marched forward; he pointed at me.*

1 Complete the sentences below by adding a related clause using a semi-colon. The first one has been done for you.
  a I have been sitting here for a long time; I feel quite cross.
  b The ball came straight towards me.
  c The weather was sunny when I walked to school.
  d Our train leaves at 8 a.m.

2 Join the eight sentences below using a semi-colon to make four new sentences. Make sure you join up the correct ones!

> Winter is cold. The man glared at me. I love it when my mum makes peanut butter sandwiches. His eyes were full of anger. I so hope she likes my new shoes. Summer is hot. She always puts one in my lunch box. She hated the last pair.

Talk Partners

In pairs, play the semi-colon game. One talk partner says a sentence, and the other has to think of an appropriate sentence which could be added using a semi-colon.

Brackets

Helpful hints

Brackets are used to separate additional information from the rest of the sentence. For example:

- Shakespeare's 'A Midsummer Night's Dream' (written in the 1590s) is still very popular today.
- The girl (aged 12) won the award for swimming.
- Mariyah (my best friend) is coming to my party on Sunday.

Each of these sentences still makes sense without the information in brackets.

1 Use the information below to write three sentences, putting one piece of information in brackets.

a 'Great Expectations' – Charles Dickens – published in 1861.

b The new shoes – made of bright red leather – were his pride and joy.

c The bus – bright yellow – took the children to the school sports day.

2 Write four sentences where brackets are used to separate additional information about:

- a date
- someone's age
- some extra information about a person
- some extra information about a place.

3 Which sentence below has used brackets incorrectly?

a I like chocolate cake (with lashings of cream).

b The athlete (from Spain) won the race.

c The boy was in danger of falling off his bike because of (his careless) behaviour.

Dashes

Helpful hints

Dashes are used to bring information to the attention of the reader. For example:

- The boy – who was only ten years old – won first prize.
- I hope – really hope – that you will come along tonight.

1 Write these five sentences so that the additional information is brought to the attention of the reader through dashes.

a   My mother cooked the dinner last night.
(a three course meal)

b   I hope to read the book by tomorrow night.
(a thousand pages long)

c   The old man pushed open the large oak door.
(with trembling hands)

d   The park was extremely crowded.
(which is enormous)

e   Maria Honorez has climbed Mount Everest.
(aged 18 years)

2 Use dashes in three sentences so that the information below is included. The first one has been done for you.

Please pick up your pen – not a pencil – and complete your writing.

- not a pencil
- carefully
- only seven years old

Try this

Conduct some research! Investigate a range of non-fiction texts such as articles, web pages and leaflets for sentences which use dashes. Copy out six examples of dashes used in a sentence. Is there another way of using the dash? Look particularly at when a single dash is used.

Using colons, semi-colons, brackets and dashes

1 Your family have won a competition entitling them to a free holiday anywhere in the world.

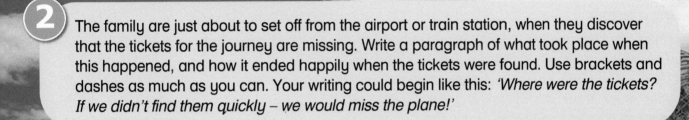

a   Decide where you would like to go. It should be somewhere all the family would enjoy!

b   Make a list of what you are going to take with you, taking care to use colons and semi-colons correctly! You could start your list like this: *'For my holiday, I need to take the following items:'*

2 The family are just about to set off from the airport or train station, when they discover that the tickets for the journey are missing. Write a paragraph of what took place when this happened, and how it ended happily when the tickets were found. Use brackets and dashes as much as you can. Your writing could begin like this: *'Where were the tickets? If we didn't find them quickly – we would miss the plane!'*

3 Write two more paragraphs. One paragraph should describe the best day of the holiday, and the other the worst. Your aim is to use a range of punctuation. This should include the following: full stop, comma, colon, semi-colon, brackets, dashes, ellipsis.

4 Write a final paragraph about the journey and arrival home. This will be more downbeat. Use the dash, brackets and ellipsis to show the change of mood. For example, *I was so sorry to leave, and wished – really wished – we could stay for an extra week (or even a day) so that we could explore more of the island.* Finish this final paragraph with an ellipsis.

What have I learnt?

Read through your writing, copy this table and check you have included the following:

Punctuation	Yes?	How many?
Colon		
Semi-colon		
Dash		
Brackets		
Ellipsis		

Unit 5 Fiction: characters and settings

Unit 5

Helpful hints

Authors are very clever! Just by writing words on a page they can create images of people and places which readers then **see**!

Extract 1:

Creating a picture

As soon as the ship docked, Yusof jumped ashore and began to explore the town, admiring mosques and palaces, peering down interesting **alleyways** and listening to strange music from behind closed doors. Quickly he found himself a room in a hostel, and was soon sitting in the inner courtyard with a cool drink in his hand and the chatter of other travellers all around him. But suddenly – just as it was time to look for some dinner – a violent wind sent the dust whirling round in furious **eddies**, the trees of the courtyard **flailed** about as if a hurricane had struck, and everything went dark. The **khan's** owner dashed out of his kitchen. "Run, sirs! Run for shelter!" he shouted. "The Giant Okab is coming..."

Adapted from The Giant Okab by Shirin Adl and Elizabeth Laird

1 Read through extract 1. Writers can make images visual by using **adjectives**. Pick out and write the adjectives from the phrases below.
- listening to strange music
- peering down interesting alleyways
- a cool drink in his hand
- a violent wind sent the dust whirling round in furious eddies

Glossary

alleyway: a narrow path or road between buildings
eddy: a current of air moving in a circular motion
flail: to wave or swing wildly
khan: an inn or hostel

2 The **choice of verbs** is important in creating a vivid picture of things happening. Write five verbs from extract 1 above that you find effective and explain why.

I can give my personal responses to reading.

I can comment on the writer's use of language, and its impact on the reader.

I know and understand how a writer creates character and setting.

Presenting characters and settings

1 Read the phrase below.

Suddenly – just as it was time to look for some dinner – a violent wind sent the dust whirling round in furious eddies, the trees of the courtyard flailed about as if a hurricane had struck, and everything went dark.

What is the effect of this phrase?

Choose two answers from this list:

- creates excitement
- creates tension
- creates anticipation
- creates interest
- creates fear.

2 Writers will often use literary devices such as similes, onomatopoeia and personification to help emphasise particular words or feelings to the reader.

In extract 1, find one example of:

a   simile
b   personification
c   onomatopoeia

Helpful hints

Similie: Where two things are compared using **as** or **like**, for example, her hand was cold like ice.

Personification: When human feelings and actions are given to objects or ideas, for example, the angry rain.

Onomatopoeia: a word which imitates the natural sound, for example, bang, hiss, crash.

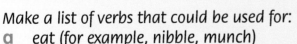

Make a list of verbs that could be used for:

a   eat (for example, nibble, munch)
b   walk (for example, stride, saunter)
c   said (for example, shriek, mutter, whisper).

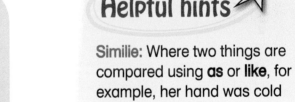

Try this

Effects writers use

1 Read extract 1 on page 62 again. Punctuation can be very useful for writers to help create an effect.

a Explain the effect of the **dash** and **ellipsis** in the extract.

b Choose your favourite sentence from extract 1 on page 62, and say why you like it so much. Write your answer like this:

The sentence I like best is ' ....
....' Because I ....
....
.........…............. .

Remember to use quotation marks to show the sentence has been taken from the extract.

2 The writer of extract 1 has created a vivid picture of the setting.

a Draw what you see described by the writer.

b What details would you include to capture the frightening atmosphere created by the writer at the end of the extract?

Helpful hints

- A **dash** is used to separate a word, phrase or clause from the rest of the sentence so that the reader really notices it, for example, I hope – really hope – you will come out tonight!
- An **ellipsis** is use to show words have been deliberately missed out for effect, for example, 'She was coming slowly towards me ...'
- **Single quotation marks** are put round a word or a phrase to show it has been taken from a text, for example, in the passage the writer tells us that Yusof 'jumped ashore and began to explore the town'.

Talk Partners

With a partner, make a list of the techniques used by writers to create an effective setting. You should try to have at least six techniques in your list.

I know and understand how an author creates setting.

I can comment on the writer's use of language, demonstrating its effect on the reader.

How an author creates setting

Extract 2:

It was a small, comfortable room with two windows. The front one looked on to the graveyard, the other to a little garden at the side. The large black **range** stood solidly in an alcove at the back wall, a thick dark pipe curving its way upward through the ceiling. Stretched out beneath the side were a few shelves filled with books, old newspapers and odds and ends, and by the front window stood a heavy wooden table and two chairs. The flagstone floor was covered in a faded crimson, green and brown rug. Willie glanced at the armchair by the range and the objects that lay on top of the small wooden table beside it: a pipe and a book.

Adapted from Goodnight Mister Tom by Michelle Magorian

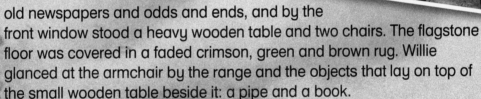

1

a   The description of the room uses adjectives to give the reader a clear picture. How many can you find?
   • If you can find 10: good.
   • If you can find 15: very good.
   • If you can find 20: excellent.

b   Give three differences between the settings described in extract 1 on page 62 and extract 2 on this page.

Glossary

range: an old fashioned cooker

How an author creates character, setting, time and mood

Outside, the frost hadn't lifted all day. It coated the inside of our window pane, so, it was a job to get a view of anything. Just to look decent, I'd kept on my best Sunday frock though the fabric was thin and I was shivering with cold. I'd even had a go at tidying my hair, and now that was escaping its plaits. Nothing was going to plan.

'For goodness sake, Tilly, do something useful', said Ma irritably, as I flopped down into my seat for the hundredth time. 'Shame you're so useless at sewing, or you could help me.'

'And take that smart frock off. It's only Pa coming home, not the Queen,' said my sister Eliza, who couldn't sew either, although no one seemed to mind about *that*. I shot her a look, but she didn't bite back. In truth, I was too **distracted** to care. Pa was due home today from a **stint** on the railways. There'd be money at last, which would put food on the table and pay the rent we owed. More importantly, he would have kisses and kind words for me.

A sudden noise and I jolted in my seat. Someone was at the front door. It wasn't a proper knock; it was a low, secret sound like an animal scratching. My heart sank. It was too quiet to be Pa. Ma was staring at the door, her lips set tight. I knew that look, and it made my heart sink more. It wasn't Pa she was thinking of, but the overdue rent and the landlord who came looking for it. Chances were it was him again.

'Tell 'im I'm not in', said Ma. 'Just do it, will you.'

I turned to Ma, 'Do I have to?'

She didn't answer.

Glossary

distracted: unable to pay attention or concentrate on something

stint: a period of work

I made for the door, and opened it just a sliver. The air coming in was bitter cold. But it wasn't the landlord who stood there. When he turned round to face me, I shut the door quick, and leaned against it hard. Will Potter. Will Potter. What was he doing here?

'Tilly!' he shouted through the keyhole. 'Come outside, won't you.'

I prayed he would go away. Eliza was looking at me, 'Who's out there, then?'

'No one much –', I muttered, but then Will Potter knocked again, a proper rat-a-tat this time so the whole world might hear it. Eliza was the first on her feet, and threw the door open wide, making Ma cry, 'Keep the heat in!'

And so Will Potter was asked inside.

Immediately, our one downstairs room looked smaller. I saw Will take in the dark beams, the threadbare rug before the hearth and the turnips in the basket in the dresser. The only tidy thing was our table, covered in neat piles of mending work that Ma took in from the village. It paid little and hurt her eyes.

He had already taken his cap off so his dark hair stood on end, and his face was one big smile. He was still shifting something about under his jacket. He opened his jacket up an inch or two. I couldn't resist a quick peep inside. There was leather, a buckle, something pale, the colour of wood. I did not have the faintest idea what it was. He must have read my frown, shifting the thing so I saw it better. Silver blades glinted back at me from the dark inside of his coat. I knew at once and my heart leapt.

Ice skates.

I looked right at him.

'Dare you', he said …

Frost Hollow Hall by Emma Carroll

I know how an author presents character.

I can comment on a writer's use of language, and how it impacts on the reader.

Character

1 Read the extract from *Frost Hollow Hall* on pages 66–67. Answer these questions about Tilly's character.

a Why is Tilly dressed in her best Sunday frock?

b What does Tilly's hair style suggest about her character?

c What is the main reason Tilly wants her father to come home?

d How does the reader know that Tilly is jealous of her sister?

e Will wants Tilly to go skating. From your knowledge of her so far, do you think she will go with him?

Helpful hints

When we meet people for the first time, we can often pick up clues about what they are like from what they are wearing, what they say and how they respond to people. Writers will give us similar sorts of clues about a character.

2 Draw Tilly and label the drawing with quotations from the extract. For example, next to her hair the quotation would be, 'I'd even had a go at tidying my hair, and now that was escaping its plaits.'

Talk Partners

Decide who is going to be Tilly, and who is going to be Will. Keeping in role, have a conversation. Is Tilly happy to agree with Will and what he wants to do? What will she (or Will) say to her mother and sister?

Setting

1 Read the extract on pages 66–67 again. How do we know that the house Tilly and her family are in has the following features? Copy and complete the table below.

Feature	Evidence from the extract
A window	
A door	
A table	
A dresser	
A rug	
A fire	

Helpful hints

Writers always give readers a picture of where a story is taking place. This is called a **setting**. Sometimes, they will give a large amount of description at once. However, often they will 'drip feed' small bits of information in, so that the reader gradually builds up a picture of the setting.

2 The writer has used adjectives to give the reader a clear picture of what is in the room.
List the five adjectives used in these sentences.

I saw Will take in the dark beams, the threadbare rug before the hearth and the turnips in the basket in the dresser. The only tidy thing was our table, covered in neat piles of mending work that Ma took in from the village.

Try this

When writers choose a particular type of weather or setting, they do so for a reason. What difference would it have made if the weather had been hot and sunny in this story?

Point of view

I know how to take account of a viewpoint in a novel, and distinguish voice of author from that of narrator.

1 Read the extract on pages 66–67 again.
Give evidence from the extract that shows Tilly:
a   loves her father
b   does not want to see Will Potter
c   is ashamed of the house she lives in.

Helpful hints

Sometimes the writer will hand over the 'voice' to a character so that they tell the story from their point of view. When this happens, we say that the story is being written in the **first person**. For example, *Just to look decent, **I'd** kept on **my** best Sunday frock …* Stories written from a first person point of view can let us into the mind of the character. This means we can see at first hand what they think and feel about things.

Writing presentation

If this extract was written from Eliza's point of view what might she want to tell the reader about Tilly? Focus on the beginning of the story only, and rewrite it from Eliza's point of view. Start it like this, *It was freezing cold, so why was Tilly wearing her best summer dress? She looked …*

2 Explicit information can be found in the extract. When there is a question which requires you to find implicit information, the answer will need to be worked out from the clues given.
a   What does Tilly's mother do to earn money? (explicit question)
b   Why is Will allowed to come into the house? (implicit question)

3 Make up two questions of your own on the extract. Focus one on explicit meaning, the other on implicit meaning.

Tip
Explicit question: These usually start with 'who, what, when'.
Implicit question: These usually start with 'why, how, if, what if'.

Word classes

Helpful hints

It is important to know how a writer uses language – especially different word classes such as nouns, verbs, adjectives, adverbs.

- A noun is somebody or something.
  For example, *man, cat, hope, Mr Banerjee, Pakistan.*
- An adjective describes somebody or something.
  For example, *busy evening; this looks good.*
- A verb is either doing or being. For example, *I ran to the shops; I am very happy.* Often verbs work together as a little group known as a **verb phrase**, '*I must be going soon.*'
- An adverb gives more meaning to a verb or another adverb.
  For example, *I really like you* or *She walks very quickly*.

1 Adverbs can do quite a lot of things in a sentence. They give more meaning about:

How?	Where?	When?	How often?
quietly	here	now	never
slowly	there	yesterday	regularly
suddenly	outside	later	frequently

Choose six adverbs from the table, and put each one in a sentence. Try to vary where you put them.

Now I will tell you.
I will tell you now.
I will now tell you.

2 Sort the following words into four different word classes:
noun, verb, adjective, adverb

am going   always   thought   soon   woman   cooked   rain
headteacher   inside   happiness   tattered   younger   happy
will be   yellow   quickly

More word classes

Now it happened that shortly after the merchant had placed his daughter in a large water-tight basket and set it adrift on the river, a handsome young prince was nearing the end of his journey to the sacred waters of the **Ganges**. Far off he saw what appeared to be a dancing star. He watched it with great interest, and when the light came closer, he turned and said to his servants, "Swim out to **yonder** floating object and bring it to me."

When the swimmers had pulled the basket to the shore a servant held the light while the prince carefully lifted the cover. He stared down at what appeared to be a large bundle of sparkling silk. Then, like a flower drawn by the sun, the maiden lifted her bowed head and gazed at her rescuers. The prince, struck dumb by surprise, looked closely into the tear-stained face and decided that she was the most beautiful **maiden** that he had ever seen. Without a word he gave her his hand and helped her from the basket.

"Maiden," he asked when he had recovered from his surprise, "why were you placed in the basket and set afloat on Mother Ganges?"

From Tales Told in India by Berta Metzger

Glossary

Ganges: a river in India, sometimes called Mother Ganges
yonder: another word for 'that', used to refer to something situated at a distance
maiden: a young woman

1. Read this extract by Berta Metzger. Nouns, adjectives, verbs and adverbs have been used to give a vivid picture of the object in the river. Find and write the following from the extract:
   a three nouns
   b three adjectives
   c three verbs
   d three adverbs.

Try this

Similes are very useful to writers as they create two pictures for the price of one! For example, 'Her hair (one picture) was **as** soft as silk.' (another picture). Similes always use 'like' or 'as' when saying that one thing is like another. For example, 'Her fingers were **like** thin sticks.'
a Can you find a simile in the extract?
b Make up your own similes for: an old tree; a long road; a high building.

I can develop imaginative detail through careful use of vocabulary.

Shades of meaning

Helpful hints

When writing, it is important to use the right **noun, adjective, verb** or **adverb**, so the right shade of meaning is conveyed. For example, if a writer wants to describe somewhere as filthy, there will be a big difference between using the adjectives 'unwashed' and 'stained'. 'Unwashed' means that something or someone looks as if it has not been washed – whereas 'stained' means something has marks which might not be removed easily! Using the right adjective is important.

1 Choose some adjectives from the box below to write four sentences about somewhere you know that is very dirty – such as a local rubbish dump or derelict building. Think about what features might be there such as litter, crumbling walls or broken furniture. Use your chosen adjectives precisely. The adjectives in **bold** can also function as verbs.

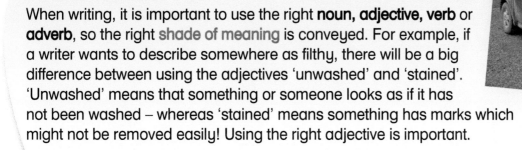

> filthy   grubby   **stained**   mucky   **tarnished**   **spoiled**
> dusty   **smudged**   **spotted**   **smeared**   greasy
> **spotted**   grimy   unwashed   **tarnished**   **spoiled**

2 Unscramble these synonyms for 'hot'.
a   grubinn
b   conchrigs
c   beltingsir
d   genetwirls
e   gilbino
f   erasing

Writing presentation

Choose two of the synonyms for 'hot' and write two to three sentences describing a very hot day in the classroom.

Did you know?

The hottest temperature on Earth was recorded on 13 September 1922 in El Azizia, Libya with a record of 136°F and 58°C!

Writing a setting

1 From the work you have covered so far, what other techniques for describing a setting would you add to those listed below?

WRITER'S TOOLBOX

Techniques for describing setting:
- colour
- adjectives
- short sentences
- similes
- •
- •

Helpful hints

A writer's 'toolbox' is a box of techniques and tricks that can be used when writing. You have explored many techniques for describing a setting effectively, so these could be put in the box and then brought out when you need to use them – just like a real writer does!

2 Begin a story which takes place in one of the following settings:
- a desert
- a derelict building
- a room in an old house.

Write a paragraph which gives the readers lots of individual detail. They should be able to see exactly what the place looks like. Use as many writers' techniques as you can!

Talk Partners

Read your description of setting to a partner, emphasising the most effective words and phrases. Doing this will ensure they are really heard!

Ask your partner:
a Which words and phrases did they find most effective?
b Were there any that could be improved?

I can use ICT effectively to prepare and present my writing.

I can vary how I speak so as to engage the listener.

Presenting your writing

1 Word process your description of a setting from page 74. When you have typed it, highlight the following word classes:

a   Yellow – all the adjectives
b   Blue – all the verbs
c   Green – all the nouns
d   Red – all the adverbs.

This will help you see whether you have a good mix of different word classes.

2 You might also want to highlight some more writers' techniques in different colours and ways. Look back at your writer's toolbox from page 74. How many of these have you used?

Writing presentation

When you have typed up your setting, illustrate it with a drawing. You might decide to give it a title. All the details in the writing should be in the drawing. Your description will then be ready to be presented or displayed.

What have I learnt?

Read through your final draft of a setting. Check that you have included the following writing techniques:

- adjectives to give a precise picture/image
- powerful verbs
- adverbs to give more information about how, where, when, how often
- alliteration   • onomatopoeia
- personification   • similes
- metaphors   • short sentences
- colours.

Creating setting and character

No glass shone in the rows of shopfronts. Pots filled with geraniums had once sat beneath the streetlamps, making the village pretty; now the pots lay destroyed, and soil had spilled onto the road, and the lampposts, which had been stately, stood in the awkward angles of shipwreck masts, glass scattered at their feet. Chiselled stones which had once made houses for people and halls for officials and pillars for the market and, in the square, a pagoda to frame the town band, now lay about in ugly piles, clogging the streets and heaped against those walls that were still standing. Here and there, lazy fires burned, feeding on window-frames and spilled fuel.

The children stepped carefully around the rubble, their footfalls making no noise, the taller walking ahead of the smaller and deciding their path.

The Midnight Zoo by Sonya Hartnett

1 Read the extract above. Re-write the setting so that it looks like it did **before** the event. It should start like this: 'Glass shone in the rows of shopfronts …'

2 Read the extract again.
a What do you think has happened to the street?
b Who are the two children?
c Why are they there?
d Where are they going?

3 From the extract, write down three sentences or phrases you find effective.

Writing presentation

Continue the story for two more paragraphs linking paragraphs together appropriately, finishing at an exciting point for the reader. Remember to use some of the techniques you have learned for creating effective characters and setting. Use the checklist on page 75 to remind you of the techniques.

I know how to present ideas about characters in drama through speech, gesture and movement.

Making drama

1 Change the three paragraphs you have written on page 76 into a play. Use the example in the Helpful hints box opposite to help you get started.

2 Rehearse the play so it is ready to be performed. Some decisions will need to be made:
- What costumes will you use? These could be simple, such as an old jacket or scarf.
- How are you going to represent the rubble and high rock sat on by the children?
- Who is going to play the parts of the two children?
- Will there be a narrator?
- How do you want the actors playing the parts of the children to speak and behave?

3 Perform the play. What went well? What could be done to improve it?

Helpful hints

Drama is different from fiction and poetry because it works through what the characters say. For example, in a book we might have: *The children stepped carefully around the rubble, their footsteps making no noise, the taller walking ahead of the smaller and deciding their path.*

In a play we might have:
Mateo *(weeping)*: I'm scared. What's happening?
Johan *(without turning round)*: Ssh, be quiet! Just follow me. We need to get out of here and towards the safe part of town.
(Both boys continue to climb over the rubble until they come to a high rock where they sit and rest.)

Techniques for reading and writing fiction

Fiction genres

Helpful hints

There are many different types and styles of fiction texts such a mystery, fantasy, and adventure. These are often referred to as genres. Each fiction genre will treat plot, character and setting in its own particular way. A science fiction story about space travel set in the future will be very different to a fairy tale about a magic quest, and set 'long, long ago'.

1 Working with a partner, copy and complete the genre table below. The first genre (science fiction) has been done for you.

Typical features	Typical plot	Typical characters	Typical setting	Typical dialogue	Anything else
Science fiction	Aliens will take over Earth. Discovery of the unknown.	Spaceship commander and crew; aliens and their leader.	In the future, for example, 2040	'I think we have a problem. An unidentified object has been spotted.'	Characters dressed in silver suits. Aliens – a mixture of human and non-human.
Fairy story					Usually begins, 'Once upon a time/ Long ago'; foolish characters learn a lesson; unrealistic, stereotypical characters.
Myth	Simple story which explains how something natural happened before human beings were on the earth, for example, How the wind learned how to blow.				
Real life adventure		People you would meet in real life. A hero or villain.			Very quick. A series of small problems build up, leading to a bigger one. Very tense and dramatic!
Suspense			Deserted building, forest or town late at night.		

I can use different genres as a model for writing.

I can create a plot and characters and build these into an extended story.

2 Which genres do these beginnings of stories belong to?

Science fiction   Real life adventure   Mystery/suspense   Myth   Fairy story

a   Miserably, Aja stared out of the rain streaked window and sighed. What was she going to do today? Suddenly, the telephone rang, its ring sharp and harsh. Who could possibly be ringing so early in the morning?

b   The giant spaceship descended silently through the thick night air, edging closer and closer to the Earth's surface ...

c   Once upon a time, a very long time ago, there was a poor boy who lived with his mother on the edge of a tumbledown village. Now, this boy was often a foolish boy. That very day ...

d   It was at the beginning of time, and long before human beings came to the Earth. There was sun, but no rain. This had become a problem.

e   A door banged. Zara jumped. What was that? Out of the silence, she heard steps. Somebody was coming closer. Somebody or something was climbing up the stairs.

3 Choose one of the beginnings of stories from activity 2. Complete the paragraph, and then go on to write two more, finishing the third paragraph at an exciting point for the reader. Include some dialogue in your writing so the characters speak to one another. Remember to use speech marks correctly, and to use a new line when there is a new speaker. For example:

'Hello, who is this?' Aja whispered, her voice thin and trembling.
'It's me,' growled the voice at the other end of the telephone.

I can create a plot and characters and build these into an extended story.

I can pay close attention to what others say, and ask and answer questions to introduce new ideas.

Improving writing

1 Read your paragraphs from activity 3 on page 79 out aloud. As you do so, think about and note down any:

a   words or expressions which need improving

b   errors in punctuation or spelling which need correcting.

Talk Partners

Ask a partner to read your paragraphs aloud, and to tell you what they thought about them.

a   What three features did they like about your story?

b   What one feature do they wish could be improved upon?

Try this

Often readers will have a favourite genre. Which type of story do you like best, and read more of? Make a list of all the books you have read in your favourite genre.

What have I learnt?

Read through your paragraphs again. Use the checklist below to help you make any final changes. Can you think about anything else you would like to add?

I have:

- included typical genre features
- written three paragraphs, linking paragraphs together appropriately
- included dialogue
- used speech marks correctly
- used an effective range of vocabulary, including some connectives
- finished my story at a tense and exciting point.

Presenting your story

1 Word process your paragraphs from page 80. The presentation of the story can be made more effective by:

a Giving it a title. This should give the reader some indication of what the story is going to be about. It should also be interesting enough to make them want to read it. For example, 'The Hidden Secrets of the Deserted House.'

b Finishing the story with an ellipsis (…).

c Using 1.5 or double line spacing.

d Using clip art to insert a picture to go with it. Add a caption underneath your picture.

2 Use the following proof-reading strategy:

Step 1 Read through your work and check you have a full stop at the end of each sentence.

Step 2 Read through your work a second time and check you have a capital letter at the start of each new sentence.

Step 3 Read through your work a third time and check that you have used the following correctly:
- commas within sentences to separate words, phrases or clauses
- question marks for questions
- exclamation marks when you need to emphasise something
- a capital letter to start a proper noun (someone's name or a place)
- speech marks around dialogue, and a new line when there is a new speaker.

Step 4 Read through your work a fourth time and check the spelling – particularly any difficult words. If you see a word that doesn't look right, underline it and then think of a strategy you could use to remind you of how it is spelt correctly. If you are unsure, use a dictionary to check the word.

Story beginnings

A

When Mary Lennox was sent to Misselthwaite Manor to live with her uncle everyone said that she was the most disagreeable looking child ever seen. It was true, too. She had a little thin face, and a little thin body, thin light hair and a sour expression.

The Secret Garden by Frances Hodgson Burnett

B

In a wild part of Western Virginia in the United States of America lived a poor old widow and her daughter. Their home was a tumble-down old shack, built near a great chasm, and miles away from any neighbours. The railway, which ran between Baltimore and Ohio, had its track close-by, and it spanned the yawning ravine by means of a high wooden bridge.

Adapted from Almost a Disaster

C

Once upon a time Anansi was walking through the forest when he saw a strange, moss-covered rock.
"How interesting!" said Anansi to himself. "Isn't this a strange moss-covered rock?" Suddenly ... KABOOM! Everything went black and Anansi fell down, fast asleep. When he woke up, Anansi rubbed his spinning head and wondered what had happened to him. "I was walking along this path," he reminded himself, "something caught my eye and I said to myself, 'Isn't this a strange moss-covered rock?' and then ..." KABOOM! Anansi fell down again and woke up about an hour later.

Adapted from Anansi and the Moss-covered Rock

D

For most of the animals of Farthing Wood a new day was beginning. The sun had set, and the hot, moistureless air was, at last, cooling a little. It was dusk, and for badger, time for activity.

The Animals of Farthing Wood by Colin Dann

E

High above the city, on a tall column, stood a statue of the Happy Prince. He was gilded all over with thin leaves of fine gold, and for eyes he had two bright sapphires and a large red ruby glowed on his sword hilt. He was very much admired.

The Happy Prince by Oscar Wilde

I can understand how to structure writing effectively.

I know how beginnings of stories are managed and then developed.

1 Beginnings to a story can start in different ways.
Read the story beginnings on page 82.
Which story begins in the following way?
   a   Description of a setting
   b   Focus on something
   c   Focus on a particular time of day
   d   Dialogue used
   e   Description of a character

2
   a   For each beginning predict what you think is going to happen next.
       How do you think each story will end?
   b   Which beginning do you like best?

Writing presentation

Use your favourite beginning as a model, and write the beginning to a story of your own.

Try this

Find out what happened at the end of story A, D or E on page 82. Was your prediction correct?

A different way to structure a story

A **flashback** is when a story refers to an earlier event, but does not tell the reader straight away what happened. They have to read on to find out!

I disappeared on the night before my 12th birthday, July 22 1988. Only now can I at last tell the whole extraordinary story. Kensuke made me promise that I would say nothing, nothing at all, until at least 10 years had passed. It was almost the last thing he said to me. I promised, and because of that promise, I had to live out a lie. I could let sleeping lies sleep on, but more than 10 years have passed now. I have done school, done college and had time to think. I owe it to my family and to my friends, all of whom I have deceived for so long, to tell the truth about my long disappearance, about how I lived to come back from the dead.

From Kensuke's Kingdom by Michael Morpurgo

1 The beginning of *Kensuke's Kingdom* begins with a flashback. Lots of clues are given to what might have happened. These clues act like narrative hooks to engage and interest the reader, and make them want to read on to find out.

a What information do we find out about the event that happened in the past? Copy and complete this table.

When did it happen?	
What happened?	
Who knows about what happened?	
Why is the event being revealed now, and not before?	

b Is the extract written in the first or third person point of view? Explain how you know this.

c Give two reasons why a reader would want to read on.

Writing a first person flashback account

When you write in the first person you will need to use these personal pronouns:

> I me you we
> them us our

1 Take the information below and use it to write a flashback beginning, just as in *Kensuke's Kingdom*. Write six sentences, and do not give too much away. You want to interest the reader enough to make them want to keep on reading. Remember to write in the first person. For example:

- 'It happened two years ago, on the day we were …

When did it happen?	Two years ago
What happened?	There has been something missing in school
Who knows about what happened?	Only the people involved in the incident
Why is the event being revealed now, and not before?	Those involved promised they would keep it a secret

Talk Partners

Read your flashback beginning to a partner. Ask:
- Do they want to read on?
- What do they think is going to happen next?

I can comment on an author's use of language and effect on the reader.

I know how to develop some imaginative detail through the careful use of vocabulary and style.

Fiction writing techniques

Helpful hints

Readers sometimes compare reading a book to watching a film. In both, seeing images are important. This means that one important technique when writing stories is to show and not tell. Readers do not need to be told. They can work out clues from a picture. Look at the difference between.

- **Tell:** *I was scared*
- **Show**: *A door banged. Rupali jumped. What was that? Out of the silence, she heard steps. Somebody was coming closer. Somebody or something was climbing up the stairs. Closer and closer, the noise of the footsteps echoing through the thick darkness of the night air.*

1 Turn each of the 'tellings' below into a 'show'.
  a   It was hot.
  b   The car is old.
  c   Her bedroom was untidy.
  d   He was angry.

2 Describe a street in a town or village when it is crowded – and when it is empty. This means you will have to write two paragraphs. You must write in such a way that you present pictures to the reader. You could draw these pictures before you start writing. Some writers think of these writing pictures as film shots.

Try this

Use a film storyboard to help you plan your writing. Divide a blank piece of paper into eight boxes. In each box do a rough drawing of a film shot. Underneath write whether it is going to be a close-up, a medium shot or a long shot.

How dialogue can be used to move the plot along

1 Look at the difference between these beginnings to a story then answer the questions that follow.

Example 1

Two girls called Aaliyah and Lucia have been asked to stay after school to do some extra work because they were naughty. When it was time to go home, they decided to take a short cut through the old school kitchen.

Helpful hints

Readers not only want to **see** what is happening, but also to **hear**. Having characters speak can make the story seem much more real. It is also a good way to make the plot move along without the writer having to tell what is happening. When the characters are speaking it is called dialogue.

Example 2

Giving her friend the widest grin, Lucia Vega threw down her pen, flipped the exercise book shut and declared triumphantly, 'Finished! I've written four whole pages. Mrs Leroy said we can go home when it was done. Are you coming?'.
Aaliyah Bergo glanced up quickly, her small eyes glinting fiercely in the late afternoon sun, 'I've been waiting for ages – and thinking', she replied, snapping her school bag firmly shut. 'Why don't we take a short cut through the old school kitchen?'

a Add two more sentences to example 1. Write in the same style.
b Add two more sentences to example 2. Write in the same style.
c What information does example 2 give you that is not in example 1?

2 Which example did you prefer – and why?

How dialogue can convey detail about character and plot

Giving her friend the widest grin, Lucia Vega threw down her pen, flipped the exercise book shut and declared triumphantly, 'Finished! I've written four whole pages. Mrs Leroy said we can go home when it was done. Are you coming?'.

Aaliyah Bergo glanced up quickly from her closed book, her small eyes glinting in the late afternoon sun, 'I've been waiting for ages – and thinking. Why don't take a short cut through the old school kitchen?'

1 Read the extracts above and explain how the words in **bold** give information about:
   a facial expressions
   b movement
   c how the characters speak.

2 Re-write each example so that the words in **bold** are replaced by 'Lucia said' and 'Aaliyah replied'. What effect does this have?

Writing presentation

Write a short conversation between two boys. One is accusing the other of taking their book. Build in some description so that the reader can **see** the boys as well as hear them speak.

I know how the author can present information about character.

More about dialogue

 1 In each of the dialogues given below, add detail on:
- who is speaking
- how they speak
- any movement
- any facial expressions.

This additional detail could be underlined or written in a different colour.

The first one has been done for you.

a Dialogues:

I'm going home.

Please don't go home.

Additional detail (in bold):

Abdul stamped his feet furiously, and threw his school bag on the ground, 'I'm going home,' **he declared, his small face tight and angry.**
His sister laughed, and moved towards him, 'Please don't go home' **she said softly, and placed her arm gently on his.**

b 'That's my book.'
'No, it's not. It's mine.'

c 'I'm not coming with you.'
'We would like you to come.'

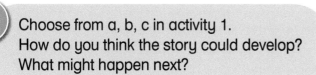

Talk Partners

Choose two lines of dialogue from activity 1 that you think have worked well. Read them to a partner. Do they agree with you?

Try this

Continue writing the example you have chosen from activity 2. Remember to add detail to the dialogue so that the characters can be seen as well as heard.

2 Choose from a, b, c in activity 1.
How do you think the story could develop?
What might happen next?

I know how the author can present information about character.

I can manage the development of an idea.

I can plan a story which has an effective plot and characters.

Writing fiction techniques

1 a Choose one of the techniques for beginning a story from the list below. This could be a technique you have worked on earlier, and which you think has worked well:

- describing a character
- describing setting
- using dialogue
- showing not telling
- focus on a time of day
- flashback
- focus on a particular feature (someone or something).

b Write the first paragraph of a story which begins with the technique you have chosen. Give it a suitable title.

2 A key feature of beginnings is that they should make the reader want to read on. Which is the better beginning and why?

Beginning 1: Her eyes glinting with determination, eight-year-old Valeria Perez pedalled furiously along the dusty road, a hat perched precariously on top of her untidy hair, giving little protection from the fierce midday sun. She had no idea where she was going, but she was determined to go somewhere.

Beginning 2: The door banged harshly in the cold evening wind, unsettling the animals in the yard. We had been waiting all evening for Samrath to come home. He had been away at school for the last year, and was due home tonight. Mother had dinner ready and we were all very excited. I hoped he would take me out horse riding tomorrow.

3

a   Draw a plan of how you think your story could develop.
Use this table to help you.

Opening paragraph:	What narrative hooks have you created so that the reader will want to read on?
2nd paragraph:	What development is there in the second paragraph? What will make the reader want to read on?
3rd paragraph:	What development is there in the third paragraph? What will make the reader want to read on?

b   How do you think the story will end? You could decide to have:

*   A closed ending where everything ends happily.
*   An open ending where the reader is not sure what might happen in the future. These sorts of endings usually finish with a rhetorical question. For example, *Who knows what will happen next?*
*   An ending which is a complete surprise to the reader and one they were not expecting.

Talk Partners

Discuss the plan of your story with a partner. Can they make any suggestions on how it could be improved?

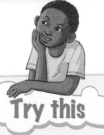

Try this

Draw a detailed plan of your story. This could be a spider diagram or a paragraph plan. Write down all your ideas, including some lines of dialogue and pieces of description you want to include. You could also add drawings of the characters or the setting.

Paragraphing a story

1 Write your story using the paragraph plan. It will be made up of four paragraphs. It is important to follow the rules for starting a new paragraph. Which three of these reasons for starting a new paragraph are incorrect?

a Change of topic
b Change of furniture
c Change of time
d Change of character
e Change of car
f Change of shoes
g Change of setting
h Change of speaker

2 When a paragraph shifts in time, the writer can use phrases such as, *The next day; Some time later; Later that day.* Check you have used suitable time phrases in your story from activity 1.

What have I learnt?

Read through your story. Use the checklist below to help you make any final changes. Think about anything else you would like to add.

I have:
- written four paragraphs, linking paragraphs together appropriately
- used suitable time phrases between paragraphs
- built in narrative hooks so that the reader wants to read on
- used an effective beginning and ending
- chosen an appropriate ending for my story
- remembered to show and not tell
- checked for the accuracy of spelling, punctuation and grammar.

Prepare, practise and improve a spoken presentation or performance

I can prepare a reading of a story for an effective performance.

 1

You are going to read your story to the rest of the class.
Practise reading your story first.

- Read it slowly, taking care to pronounce each word carefully – especially the beginning and ends of words.
- As you read, be aware of any punctuation marks, taking a slight pause when there is a comma or full stop.
- Remember to change your voice when there is a question or exclamation mark.
- Decide which words or phrases you want to emphasise.

When you read your story to the class remember to keep the copy of your story away from your face so that you can be heard clearly.

Fiction

Read the extract and answer the questions which follow.

Extract from Bella's Den

The narrator and her friend Bella have persuaded their parents to let them sleep out in the garden. Bella has dared the narrator to go into the woods so that they can stay overnight in a den Bella has built under a large tree …

I flopped through the farmyard after her till I'd worked my feet properly into the wellies, ran over the bridge and up the lane. I heard my sleeping bag rip a bit on the barbed wire and reminded myself to look for any torn bits on the fence next day. It would never do for us to leave tracks behind us. Then I lost my footing and slid all the way down the bank. I'm proud to say I didn't yell out. My sleeping bag finally fell off when I was crossing the river, and I stung myself on some nettles as I was trying to rescue it. But it was all worth it, every bit of agony was worth it, because of what happened next.

We must have been in the den for nearly an hour. There wasn't room for us to both lie down so we were sitting crouched together with Bella's sleeping bag pulled across us both. We were both staring out into the night. It was so dark then that it didn't seem to have any depth. It was like a dark curtain, just too far away to reach out and touch. Then the moon slid away from the clouds and it was suddenly as clear as day. And I think I was first to see. I was looking at the big mound below the den, and thinking how it made it look like a theatre with the stage lights on, and how deep and black the holes were, when I caught sight of a movement. I touched Bella's arm and she let out a little breath of, yes, she'd seen it too.

It was a fox. He seemed to grow out of the darkness of the hole, and then took shape as the moon lit him. He stood as if he had been turned to stone, and he was staring right at our den, right through the leaf strands, right at me. He was locked right in to me, reading the thoughts in my mind, and I daren't move or breathe, I daren't do anything but stare back at him, till my eyes were blurring. I thought I would pass out with holding myself so still, and my skin was ice-cold, frozen cold with fear.

Bella's Den by Berlie Doherty

1 a   Why does the narrator say she '**flopped** through the farmyard after her?'   (1)

   b   Who is the 'her' referred to?   (1)

2   How do we know that the den is some way away from the garden?   (1)

3   Find evidence from the extract which shows the narrator has lost her sleeping bag.   (1)

4   How do we know that the den is uncomfortable?   (1)

5   What happens so that the narrator can see in the dark?   (1)

6   Where does the fox come from and what does it do?   (2)

7   Give the meaning of the words underlined so that they mean the same as in the passage.

   a   'so we were sitting <u>crouched</u> together'

   b   'till my eyes were <u>blurring</u>'   (2)

8   'He stood as if he had been turned to stone.' Explain what this shows about the movement of the fox.   (1)

9   Give two words or phrases from the extract which suggest a drama performance.   (2)

10   Find one metaphor in the passage and explain what it means.   (2)

11   Why are the pronouns 'me', 'I', 'him', 'he' used so much in the last paragraph?   (1)

12   Choose the genre of the extract.
   a   Real life adventure
   b   Horror
   c   Fairy tale
   d   Legend
   e   Biography   (1)

13   Whose point of view does the story focus on and how do we know?   (2)

14   The passage builds up to the appearance of the fox. Which paragraph has **less** happening in it and why?   (1)

Non-fiction

Read the extract and answer the questions which follow.

Foxes

Red foxes live around the world in many diverse habitats including forests, grasslands, mountains, deserts, farms and even built-up areas in towns. The ability of the red fox to adapt to different environments has earned it a legendary reputation for intelligence and cunning.

Their diet can be flexible and will usually include insects, slugs, worms, small rodents – and anything that can be raided from our rubbish. Food is usually hunted for during the night or in the early morning hours.

At birth, red foxes are actually brown or grey. A new red coat usually grows in by the end of the first month, but some red foxes are golden, reddish-brown, silver or even black. The foxes usually hunt alone but live in family groups consisting of a dog with a vixen who can have a litter of four to five cubs. Both parents care for their young through the summer before the cubs leave in the autumn to live on their own. During the winter months the fox spends its time in its den, which is always near a source of water – such as stream or a pond.

Like a cat's, the thick tail of the fox aids its balance, but it has other uses as well. The tail is used by the fox as a flag to communicate with other foxes. Foxes also signal to each other by making scent posts – leaving their smell on trees or rocks to announce their presence.

Foxes have adapted well to life in towns over the last 50 years, and are found across London and other cities in the UK. When in urban areas, foxes adopt an almost exclusively nocturnal life in order to avoid association with humans. They prosper because they find plentiful food and shelter in our gardens, yards and other open spaces.

1   Give another word for 'diverse' in the first sentence.   (1)

2   Give two reasons why the fox has succeeded as a species.   (2)

3   Give evidence to show that foxes are involved in the upbringing of their young.   (1)

4   Are all foxes red? Support your answer with a quotation from the extract.   (1)

5   In what two ways do foxes communicate with each other?   (2)

6   Which word shows that foxes are animals that normally appear at night?   (1)

7   Why are we less likely to see a fox in the summer?   (1)

8   Explain the meaning of the phrases underlined so that they have the
    same meaning as in the passage.

    a   a <u>legendary reputation</u> for intelligence and cunning

    b   to <u>avoid association</u> with humans   (4)

9   Suggest a suitable sub-heading for each of paragraphs 2, 3 and 4.   (2)

10 The extract uses facts. Give one example of a fact from the passage.   (1)

11 Re-write the third paragraph to include the main points in no more
    than 40 words.   (4)

Thinking more about poetry

I can read and interpret poems.

I can understand that when a poem is written will make a difference to how we understand it today.

'Silver' was written by the English poet, Walter de la Mare, who lived from 1873 to 1956. Some of the words in the poem are not words we would use today. The term given to these words is **archaic.** Read the poem aloud, emphasising the words underlined.

Silver

<u>Slowly, silently</u>, now the <u>moon</u>
Walks the night in her <u>silver</u> **shoon**;
<u>This</u> way, and <u>that</u>, she <u>peers</u>, and <u>sees</u>
<u>Silver fruit</u> upon <u>silver trees</u>;
<u>One</u> by <u>one</u> the **casements** <u>catch</u>
Her <u>beams</u> beneath the <u>silvery</u> **thatch**;
<u>Couched</u> in his <u>kennel</u>, like a <u>log,</u>
With <u>paws</u> of <u>silver</u> sleeps the <u>dog</u>;
From their <u>shadowy</u> **cote** the <u>white breasts peep</u>
Of <u>doves</u> in <u>silver feathered sleep</u>
A <u>harvest mouse</u> goes <u>scampering</u> by,
With <u>silver claws,</u> and <u>silver eye</u>;
And <u>moveless fish</u> in the water <u>gleam,</u>
By <u>silver reeds</u> in a <u>silver stream</u>.

Glossary

shoon: shoes
casements: windows
thatch: roof made of straw
cote: a small shelter for doves

Understanding poetry

1 The poem, 'Silver' on page 98 uses a very clear rhyming pattern. For example, 'sees' and 'trees'.
   a   Write down the last word in each line.
   b   What **pattern** of rhyme has been used by the poet?

I can identify the sound features in a poem.

2 The poem has some quite distinctive sound features. Copy and complete this table and give an explanation of the different sound features. The first one has been done for you.

Sound feature	Example	Explanation
Rhyme	*moon/shoon*	When words sound the same as each other.
Alliteration	*slowly, silently*	

Try this

Find two more examples in the poem of alliteration.

Literary techniques in poetry

Helpful hints

Poets use techniques to help create pictures in the reader's mind. These include: repetition, personification, simile and metaphor.

- **Repetition:** when words or phrases are deliberately repeated so as to bring them to the attention of the reader.
- **Personification:** when human qualities are given to an object or an animal. For example, *The light of the moon softly tiptoed through my window.*
- **Simile:** when something is likened to something else, and is introduced by 'like' or 'as'. For example, *The moon was like a pale face.*
- **Metaphor:** when something is likened to something else but does so directly without using 'like' or 'as'. For example, *The moon is a pale face.*

1 Read the poem on page 98 again.
  a Count the number of times the word 'silver' has been used in the poem.
  b Why has it been used so many times?
  c What is the name of this technique?

2 From the poem find an example of each of the following techniques:
  a Personification (Hint: *Walks …*)
  b Simile (Hint: *Crouched …*)
  c Metaphor (Hint: *Of doves*)

Talk Partners

Check your answers to questions 1 and 2 with a partner. Working together, list the names of the animals referred to in the poem.

Writing presentation

Choose your favourite image/line from the poem and copy it out in your best handwriting. Add a drawing which illustrates the line you have chosen.

I can write with a clear viewpoint and show I have a personal voice.

I can develop an idea imaginatively through careful use of vocabulary and style.

I can write a poem!

1 You are going to write a poem.

a   Choose from one of the following topics:
- rain
- sun
- wind
- snow
- fog

b   Gather your material for the poem as follows. You will need a highlighter or coloured pen.

- Brainstorm all the images, ideas, memories, thoughts and ideas you have on your chosen topic. Try to fill a whole page in your exercise book.
- Now sort and organise these. What is your poem going to be about? For example, a very rainy day you remember; the heat of the midday sun; the power of a strong wind; a snowstorm; a foggy evening. In one colour, highlight those ideas which fit together. You may need to add some more ideas.
- Now decide how you are going to organise your poem. What is going to come first? How is the poem going to develop and then end? For example, if your chosen topic is rain, the poem could start with a little rain, getting worse, and then stopping.

c   Write at least 10–12 lines. Decide whether you are going to divide the poem into verses or not.

d   Try to include at least one example from this list: simile, metaphor, personification, repetition.

e   Read through your poem – improving where you can and cutting ideas that don't seem to work.

f   Give your poem a title. The reader must be clear on what the poem is going to be about.

Sounds are very important in a poem. Try to include an example of alliteration and rhyme in your poem.

Try this

Comparing poetry

The Whistling Wind

The wind whistles overhead,
now loud, now low,
sounding rather **melancholy**,
rather **foreboding**.

An old man totters past me,
his hand holding on tightly
to his thick, cotton-padded cap
while the wind goes on whistling . . .

The wind whistles inside my ears,
now strong, now weak,
sounding rather solemn,
rather wild.

A child coming home from school
runs past me, laughing with delight;
a handful of coloured paper scraps
at once dances through the air
while the wind goes on whistling . . .

Suddenly, I feel an inexpressible joy:
my black hair
is ruffled in the wind,
is singing in the wind.

By Wang Xiaoni

The Wind
Who has seen the wind?
Neither I nor you;
But when the leaves hang trembling
The wind is passing through.
Who has seen the wind?
Neither you nor I;
But when the trees bow down their heads
The wind is passing by.

By Christina Rossetti

Glossary

melancholy: feeling of sadness
foreboding: feeling that something bad is going to happen

I can identify similar features in poems.

I can discuss and express what I like about language, style and themes in a poem.

The language of poetry

Talk Partners

Read the two poems on page 102. Both poems are about the wind. Some features are the same, but others are very different. The exploration of differences and similarities of texts is called comparison. Working with a partner, write down your answers to these questions.

a   Which poem is shorter?
b   Which poem describes the sound of the wind?
c   Which poem questions who sees the wind?
d   What effect does the wind have on the poet at the end of `The Whistling Wind´?
e   Both poems describe the effects of the wind (either on the landscape or people). Find an example of the effects of the wind in `The Wind´ and `The Whistling Wind´.

1   Read the poems again.

a   Which two features are similar and different in the two poems?
b   Which poem do you prefer? Give a reason why.

2   Look at these extracts taken from the two poems. Then choose one and draw a picture of what you think it is about.

Suddenly, I feel an inexpressible joy:
my black hair
is ruffled in the wind,
is singing in the wind.

Who has seen the wind?
Neither you nor I;
But when the trees bow down their heads
The wind is passing by.

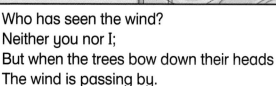

I can respond with a personal response to a poem, using close references to the text.

I know how words and sounds can have an effect in poems.

I can read and interpret poems which have implicit meaning.

Poetry which tells a story

The Listeners

"Is there anybody there?" said the Traveller,
Knocking on the moonlit door;
And his horse in the silence champed the grass
Of the forest's ferny floor;
And a bird flew up out of the turret
Above the Traveller's head:
And he smote upon the door again a second time;
"Is there anybody there?" he said.
But no one descended to the Traveller;
No head from the leaf-fringed **sill**
Leaned over and looked into his grey eyes,
Where he stood **perplexed** and still.

Glossary

sill: window sill
perplexed: puzzled
dwelt: lived
cropping: cutting (eating)
'neath: beneath
spake: an archaic word meaning 'spoke'
Ay: an archaic word meaning 'Yes'
turf: grass

But only a host of phantom listeners
That **dwelt** in the lone house then
Stood listening in the quiet of the moonlight
To that voice from the world of men:
Stood thronging the faint moonbeams on the dark stair,
That goes down to the empty hall,
Hearkening in an air stirred and shaken
By the lonely Traveller's call.
And he felt in his heart their strangeness,
Their stillness answering his cry,
While his horse moved, **cropping** the dark **turf**,
'Neath the starred and leafy sky;
For he suddenly smote on the door, even
Louder, and lifted his head:—
"Tell them I came, and no one answered,
That I kept my word," he said.
Never the least stir made the listeners,
Though every word he **spake**
Fell echoing through the shadowiness of the still house
From the one man left awake:
Ay, they heard his foot upon the stirrup,
And the sound of iron on stone,
And how the silence surged softly backward,
When the plunging hoofs were gone.

Walter de la Mare

The language of poetry

1 Copy and complete the table by matching each word from the poem with the correct meaning.

Word	Meaning
turret	banged
champed	crowding
smote	small tower
hearkening	ghostly
phantom	listening
thronging	munched

Helpful hints

'The Listeners' was written a long time ago, so it has some words we would not use today. The meaning of these words can often be worked out from the rest of the sentence.

2 Put these sentences in the order they happen in the poem.
a   Again no one answers.
b   On the final occasion he says he has come and kept his word.
c   He knocks the door for a second time.
d   He knocks on the door for a third time.
e   A traveller knocks on the door.
f   The traveller rides off.
g   He asks if anyone is in.
h   No one answers.

3 The poem is set in a forest late at night. This helps to make it more mysterious. Give two words or phrases from the poem which show that:
a   it is late at night
b   the setting is in a forest.

Thinking more about 'The Listeners'

I can listen to what others say, and ask and answer questions which introduce new ideas.

1 Read the poem on pages 104–105 again.

a Write the headings 'Outside' and 'Inside'. Underneath each write examples from the poem. For example, the Traveller and the horse would be outside, the empty hall inside.

b Suggest another title for the poem.

Talk Partners

Working as a group, each person must put forward their thoughts on who they think the listeners are, and why they do not answer the door.

Did you know?

Walter de la Mare's (1873–1956) first job was an accountant with an oil company before he became a writer and poet. He wrote over 100 ghost stories, but is best remembered for his works for children and the poem 'The Listeners'.

2 Draw an illustration to go with the poem. Look at what the other learners in the group have drawn. How are they different to yours?

Try this

In 'The Listeners', pronouns are sometimes used instead of names. List the pronouns used in the poem on pages 104–105 which refer to the listeners, for example, 'their'.

I understand how words and expression changes over time.

I know that some words can come from other languages and have different origins.

I know that when a poem is written will make a difference to how we understand it today.

How language has changed over time

The poems, 'Silver' and 'The Listeners' were written over a hundred years ago. Both use words and expressions that we no longer use today such as 'shoon' (shoes) and 'spake' (spoke).

Here are four examples from literature which show how the English language has developed and changed over time.

Example 1: Middle English 1100–1500	
In the 15th century, Geoffrey Chaucer wrote a poem called 'The Canterbury Tales'. This poem was about travellers who told one another stories on a journey to Canterbury.	
Original language	**How we would write and say it now**
Whan that the Knyght had thus his tale ytoold, In al the route nas ther yong ne oold That he ne seyde it was a noble storie And worthy for to drawen to memorie.	When the knight had told his tale Everyone on the journey, young or old Said it was a good story And worth remembering.

Example 2: Early Modern English 1500–1700	
In the 16th and early 17th century, William Shakespeare wrote many plays. One well-known play is 'The Tempest', which is set on a desert island. In this extract, a spirit called Ariel is talking to his master, Prospero.	
Original language	**How we would write and say it now**
I prithee, Remember I have done thee worthy service, Told thee no lies, made thee no mistakings, served Without or grudge or grumblings.	Listen I have been a good servant for you Not told any lies, and made no mistakes and served Without any complaints.

Example 3: Modern English 1700–1950	
Gulliver's Travels was a novel written by Jonathan Swift in the 18th century. Gulliver has been shipwrecked, and ended up stranded on a beach. When he comes round, he finds himself tied to the ground, with something very strange happening …	
Original language	**How we would write and say it now**
In a little time I felt something alive moving on my left leg, which advancing gently forward over my breast, came almost up to my chin; when, bending my eyes downwards as much as I could, I perceived it to be a human creature not six inches high.	Gradually, I felt something gently moving over my chest and coming up to my chin. When I looked down, I saw it was a human creature no bigger than six inches high. 

Example 4: Modern English Today 1950 TO PRESENT DAY	
Here is an extract from the well-known children's book, *The BFG* by Roald Dahl. This was written in 1982.	
She reached out for her glasses that lay on the chair beside her bed. They had steel rims and very thick lenses, and she could hardly see a thing without them. She put them on, then slipped out of bed and tip-toed over to the window.	It would seem very clear to us today what the author means!

1. Read example 1 Middle English, aloud. Then, the 'e' at the end of the word would be pronounced, as would the 'K' at the beginning of a word!

2. Give one difference between Early Modern English (1500–1700) and Modern English (1700–1950) and one feature that has stayed the same.

3. Read example 4. What do you think the English language will be like 50 years from now? Will it be the same or will there be some changes from Modern English?

I know that some words can come from other languages and can have different origins.

I know that words and expressions change over time.

Language change

1 Using archaic words from the list in the Helpful hints box opposite, write three sentences telling a friend about a super new shop you have just been to.

2 Copy and match the words below with their original meaning, then check an etymological dictionary to see if you were correct. This dictionary tells you about the history of words. You will find an online etymological dictionary on the internet.

Awful	a child of either gender
Bravery	a perfect copy
Girl	something wonderful, amazing
Counterfeit	showy
Tell	count

Helpful hints

Many words we have used today have changed a great deal over time. For example, 'nice' once meant ignorant or unaware. Today it means something quite different! Here are some words that were used long ago. These are referred to as **archaic**.

- anon – at once
- beforetime – before
- gadzooks – oh my goodness
- hark – pay close attention
- hither – to this place
- peradventure – perhaps
- yonder – over there.

Talk Partners

With a partner, make a list of six new words you think would have been added in the last ten years. Check an etymological dictionary to see if you were right!

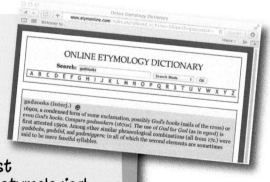

ONLINE ETYMOLOGY DICTIONARY

Did you know?

Every ten years, the Merriam Webster dictionary is updated. Their 11th edition for 2003 included some 10,000 new words along with 100,000 new meanings to words already existing and another 225,000 definitions that needed changing! In 2014 over 150 new words and definitions were added.

Words borrowed from other countries

Helpful hints

The English language has many words which have come from other languages. These have been borrowed at different times in the past, and have become such a part of the fabric of the language that we think of them as English. For example: 'duvet' was originally a French word and 'grammar' was originally a Greek word.

1 All these words ending in 'et' are French words.

> duvet   bracket   ballet   blanket   sachet
> trumpet   cabaret   banquet   scarlet   bouquet

Sort them into a table like this. The first one has been done for you.

The 'et' sounds like 'ay' in 'say'	The 'et' sounds like 'et' in 'let'
duvet	*bracket*

2 Many of our words have their origin in Greek root words. What are the English words based on these roots?
a *metron* – measure (begins with 'm' and ends in 're')
b *pathos* – suffering (begins with 'p' and ends in 'ic')
c *gramma* – letter/something written (begins with 'g' and ends in 'r')
d *spharia* – globe/ball (begins with 's' and ends in 're')

3 Below are some Italian and Spanish words. The Italian words are to do with the music and the arts. The Spanish words are to do with exploration such as travel by ship and discovery of different food. Copy the table and sort the words into the correct column.

Words borrowed from Italy	Words borrowed from Spain

> opera   piano   soprano   tomato   potato   banana   hurricane   galleon   aria

More literary techniques

Song of a Blue Mountain Stream

In a **cleft** remote
Where white mists float
Around Blue Mountain's Peak,
I rise unseen
Beneath the screen
Of fog-clouds **dank** and bleak;
I trickle, I flow
To the hills below
And vales that lie far under,
From babblings low
I louder grow,
I shout, I roar, I thunder.

I fall with a rush
In the morning hush
While the mountain sleeping lies,
There swift I sleep –
Here slow I creep,
Till the sound of my **motion** dies:
Oh! I rejoice
In the night wind's voice
As soft it kisses my stream,
And dance and glimmer
And glance and shimmer
Where moonlit reaches gleam.

With ice-cold wave
I gently **lave**
The flowers as I wander,
I gleam and glide
'Neath mountain pride,
I murmur and **meander**
Thro' fern-arched **dells**
Where fairy-bells
And violets scent the air,
While calls above
The soft blue dove
Or lone-voiced **solitaire**.

And here I crash
With silver flash
Over a mighty **crag**,
And the echoes ring
As I headlong fling
The trees I downward drag –
Till last I pour
With deafening roar,
A mountain stream no longer,
O'er plains below,
And seawards flow
A river broad and stronger.

By Reginald M. Murray

Glossary

a cleft: a narrow opening in a rock
dank: damp and cold
motion: a movement
lave: to flow along or against
meander: to follow a winding course

dells: a secluded small valley
solitaire: a type of bird found in Jamaica
crag: a steep, rugged rock
O'er: over

I can respond with a personal response to a poem, using close references to the text.

I can comment on a poet's use of language, and its effect on the reader.

More literary techniques

1

a The poem on page 112 personifies a mountain stream. It is written as if the stream is talking to the reader. What pattern of rhyme has been used in each verse of the poem?

b Where is the source of the mountain stream?

c What happens to the stream in the last verse of the poem?

d *With ice-cold wave I gently lave The flowers as I wander.* Explain what this line of the poem means.

2 Match the sentences/phrases with the correct literary technique.

a *The trees I downward drag –*

b *Oh! I rejoice In the night wind's voice As soft it kisses my stream,*

c *And here I crash With silver flash Over a mighty crag,*

| alliteration |
| onomatopoeia |
| personification |

3 Read the two poems below. Make up two questions on each poem about what they mean, and then three questions about techniques such as repetition, metaphor, personification and alliteration. Give a partner these to answer.

Fog

The fog comes
on little cat feet.
It sits looking
over harbour and city
on silent haunches
and then moves on.

Carl Sandburg

House Fear

Always – I tell you – this they learned –
Always at night when they returned
To the lonely house from far away
To lamps unlighted and fire gone grey,
They learned to rattle the lock and key
To give whatever might chance to be
Warning and time to be off in flight;
And preferring the out to the indoor night
They learned to leave the house door wide
Until they had lit the lamp inside.

Robert Frost

Looking at language

Adjectives and adverbs

Helpful hints

An adjective gives more information about what or how something looks or feels.
A simple sentence can be made more detailed by adding adjectives and **adverbs**.

The man felt hungry.
|
adjective

The old man felt **extremely** hungry.
| | |
adjective   **adverb** adjective

The old man felt **extremely** hungry and tired.
| | | |
adjective   **adverb** adjective adjective

1 Find and underline the adjectives in these sentences.

a The weather was cold and rainy.
b The football players felt depressed after the game.
c Seth was tired and Rianna was hungry.
d The red car was brand new.
e Tomorrow is going to be nice and sunny.

2 Extend the simple sentences below. Vary the adjectives and adverbs used.
The first one has been done for you.

		Add an adjective and an adverb	Add another adjective
a	The child was thirsty.	*The young child was **very** thirsty.*	*The young child was **very** thirsty and hungry.*
b	The girl felt upset.		
c	The table was new.		
d	The puppy was agitated.		

Talk Partners

Share your sentences with a partner. Ask them to choose the most effective one. Write two more sentences which follow the same sentence structure.

Adverbs

Helpful hints

Adverbs give more information about how, how often, when and where.

- An adverb of manner answers the question 'How' or 'How often'?
- An adverb of time answers the question 'When'?
- An adverb of place answers the question 'Where'?

Adverbs can go in different positions in a sentence. Where they are placed will have an effect. Look at where the adverb has been placed in these three sentences.

- **Slowly,** the old man trudged home.
- The old man **slowly** trudged home.
- The old man trudged home **slowly**.

You will notice **'slowly'** has less effect in the second sentence.

1 Copy the adverb in each sentence and identify if it is an adverb of manner, time or place.

   a   The man was running very quickly.
   b   Will you be there?
   c   Tomorrow I am playing football.
   d   We looked everywhere for the cat.
   e   We go swimming regularly.
   f   Now is the time to go.
   g   She was so cross.

2 Make sentences with the adverbs you underlined in activity 1 and use them at the beginning, middle and end of your sentences.

Try this

Use these adverbs at the beginning, middle and end of a sentence:
- frequently
- yesterday
- here

Prepositions

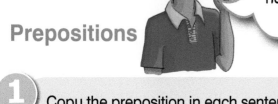

> I know what a preposition is and how it is used in a sentence.

1 Copy the preposition in each sentence.
  a   There were five apples in the bowl.
  b   The boy stared insolently at the woman.
  c   The old man walked slowly across the road.
  d   The dustbin is behind the house.
  e   The children wandered through the woods.
  f   The ants were under a stone.
  g   Many houses were damaged during the storm.

Helpful hints

Prepositions are words which show the relationship between one noun/pronoun and another. They often tell us about position. For example, I placed the dish **on** the table.

2 Copy and complete these sentences with a suitable preposition.
  a   I put the butter _____ the fridge.
  b   The dog ran _____ the path.
  c   Can you please be here at _____ 6 o'clock.
  d   I would like a kilo _____ apples, please.
  e   I will meet you _____ New York.

3 A prepositional phrase starts with a preposition. It can be used along with adjectives and adverbs to provide detail in a sentence. Look at these three sentences.

  • The old man in hospital felt **extremely** hungry and tired.
      adjective   prepositional   **adverb** adjective   adjective
                      phrase

  • She **carefully** placed a heavy lamp near the bed.
      adverb   adjective   prepositional phrase

  • At the back of the drawer, the young girl discovered her lost silver coloured party dress.
      prepositional phrase   adjective   adjective

  a   Re-write the three sentences so that the prepositional phrase is in a different position – either at the beginning, middle or end.
  b   When should a comma be used to mark off the prepositional phrase – beginning, middle or end of the sentence?

Phrases and clauses

Position of phrases and clauses

Sometimes we want to save a piece of information and not let the reader have it until the end of the sentence:

- *The child skipped home, **feeling happy.***
- *I hope to see you next week, **all being well.***

Or we may want to put the information at the beginning of the sentence:

- ***Feeling happy,** the child skipped home.*
- ***All being well,** I hope to see you next week.*

Finite clauses must contain a verb which shows tense. For example:

- ***Is** it **raining**?* (present tense)
- *I **spoke** to Peter last night.* (past tense)

Non-finite clauses contain a verb which does not show tense. We usually understand the time referred to from the context of the main clause. For example:

- *She left the party and went home, **not having anyone to talk to**.*

1 Write out two sentences so that these clauses are used at the beginning **and** at the end of the sentence. Use a comma to mark the clause off from the rest of the sentence. You could highlight the commas in a different colour.

  a Feeling sad
  b Trembling with excitement
  c Running fast
  d Walking briskly

2 Use these clauses at the beginning and end of a sentence:
  a Hoping she wouldn't be found out
  b Full of excitement
  c Upset and angry

3 Make up three sentences of your own which start with a non-finite clause. Remember to use a comma to mark the clause off from the rest of the sentence.

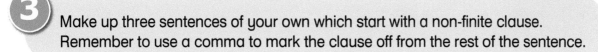

I am aware of how a writer's choice of sentence structure can have an effect.

I know how to use complex sentences and manipulate them for effect.

I can be accurate when using punctuation to mark out the meaning in complex sentences.

The position of clauses in a sentence

Helpful hints

When writing, you can make a decision whether to have a clause at the beginning of a sentence. A clause is a group of words with a verb.

A **fronted clause** is a subordinate clause placed at the beginning of a sentence.

- He liked football although he found it difficult.
  → Although he found it difficult, he liked football.
- He was tired of waiting on his own.
  → Tired of waiting on his own, he phoned a friend.
- She was hoping he would come.
  → Hoping he would come, she tidied the house.

Notice how the two fronted non-finite clauses in the second and third examples need the addition of another clause so that the sentence works and make sense!

1 Change these sentences so that they start with a fronted clause. Remember to use a comma to mark off the fronted clause from the rest of the sentence.

a I will come to see you if you promise to be very well behaved.

b The girl felt exhausted by the climb up the mountain. *(You need to add another clause)*

c The man was shopping for a new coat. *(You need to add another clause)*

2 a Write six sentences about what happened today or yesterday during school break. For example, 'I ate my chocolate bar and had a drink, and then went to play with my best friend, Louie. We talked about what we saw last night on the television. Natalie came running up to us and …'

b Now re-write the sentences, changing as many sentences as you can so that they start with a fronted clause. For example, 'Having eaten my chocolate bar, I decided to go and play with my best friend, Louie.'
You will find that you add more details in the second version!

Active and passive verbs

Helpful hints

A verb is active when the subject of the sentence performs the action.
A verb is passive when the subject of the sentence has the action done to it.

* *Senara is speaking to Beatrice.*

    active

* *Beatrice is being spoken to by Senara.*

    passive

Often the passive voice is used if the action is more important than the agent:
This school was built in 2000.
A school inspection has taken place.
The important thing is what happened, not who did it.
The passive voice is important when you want to draw attention to information, such as in public notices, announcements and instructions.
For example:

* *German is only spoken here.*

    passive

* *We only speak German here.*

    active

1 Change these sentences from the active into the passive.

   a   Jun is eating a sandwich.
       A sandwich is _____
   b   Jian is speaking to Hulin about football.
       Hulin is _____
   c   My father is cooking a meal.
       A meal is _____

2 Change the following sentences into the passive voice so there is **no agent** or **subject.**

   a   We do not allow food to be eaten on these premises. No food _____
   b   He broke the window with the ball. The window _____
   c   The school does not allow running in the corridors.

Talk Partners

With a talk partner play an active and passive game. One partner has to say a sentence about something that is happening in class. This will be in the active voice. The other has to change this into the passive. The active sentences need to have a direct object. For example:

* Fred is writing a story. (active)
* The story is being written by Fred. (passive)

All these sentences will show the agent.

Writing presentation

Write down six rules from your school. Write these in the active voice showing the agent and then in the passive voice without the agent.
For example:

* The headteacher says children must not run along corridors. (active)
* Running along corridors is not allowed. (passive)

Little House on the Prairie

In the thin dark morning Ma gently shook Mary and Laura till they got up. In firelight and candlelight she washed and combed them and dressed them warmly. Over their long red flannel underwear she put wool petticoats and wool dresses and long wool stockings. She put coats on them, and their rabbit skin hoods and their red yarn mittens.

Everything from the little house was in the wagon, except the beds and tables and chairs. They did not need to take these, because Pa could always make new ones.

There was thin snow on the ground. The air was still and cold and dark. The bare trees stood up against the frosty stars. But in the east the sky was pale and through the grey woods came lanterns with wagons and horses, bringing Grandpa and Grandma and aunts and cousins.

Mary and Laura clung tightly to their rag dolls and did not say anything. The cousins stood round and looked at them. Grandma and all the aunts hugged and kissed them, and hugged and kissed them again, saying goodbye.

Pa hung his gun to the wagon bows inside the canvas top, where he could quickly reach it from his seat. He laid his **fiddle** between pillows, where the jolting would not hurt it.

The uncles helped him hitch the horses to the wagon. All the cousins were told to kiss Mary and Laura, so they did. Pa picked up Mary and then Laura and set them on a bed in the back of the wagon. He helped them climb up to the wagon seat, and Grandma reached up and gave her Baby Carrie. Pa swung up and sat beside Ma, and Jack, the bulldog, went under the wagon.

So they all went away from the little log house. The shutters were over the windows so the little house could not see them go. It stayed there inside the log fence, behind the big oak trees that in the summer time had made green roofs for Mary and Laura to play under. And that was the last of the little house.

They drove a long way through the snowy woods, till they came to the town of Pepin. Mary and Laura had seen it once before, but it looked different now. The door of the store and the doors of all the houses were shut, the tree stumps were covered with snow and no little children were playing outdoors. Only two or three men in long boots and fur caps and bright **plaid** coats were to be seen.

Laura Ingalls Wilder

Glossary

fiddle: a violin
plaid: checked

I can give my comments on the writer's use of language in a story, including my personal response.

1 Read through the extract on pages 120–121. It is about a 19th-century family who decide to leave their small house in the American mid-west to find a better place to live. Answer these questions:

a   Write down the names of the five family members in the wagon.

b   Find two pieces of evidence which show that Pa was a capable and dependable man.

c   How does the reader know that the grandparents are sad to see the family go?

2 Write down four adjectives the writer has used to show that the morning is chilly and gloomy.

3

a   Read through the first paragraph and write down the adjectives and adverbs used.

b   What do the use of adjectives and adverbs suggest about the relationship between Ma and her two daughters?

Talk Partners

Compare your lists of adjectives and adverbs. Are they the same?

4

Read this extract from the text below. The rest of the extended family comes to say goodbye to Laura and Mary.

Mary and Laura clung tightly to their rag dolls and did not say anything. The cousins stood round and looked at them. Grandma and all the aunts hugged and kissed them, and hugged and kissed them again, saying goodbye.

a   Although Mary and Laura do not speak, which adverb has been used to show they might be upset?

b   Why has the non-finite clause, 'saying goodbye' been placed at the end of the sentence?

5   Read this extract.

He helped them climb up to the wagon seat, and Grandma reached up and gave her Baby Carrie. Pa swung up and sat beside Ma, and Jack, the bulldog, went under the wagon.

a   Write down the five prepositions used.

b   Why are there so many?

Did you know?

Laura Ingalls Wilder was born in a little log house in the mid-west in 1867. Her childhood was spent travelling through Native American territory in a covered wagon. Her own daughter encouraged her to write about it. The book, *Little House on the Prairie,* was so successful that it developed into a series of books.

123

Standard English

Helpful hints

Standard English is the accepted way of speaking and writing that most people would agree to be the normal and correct one to be used in formal situations. **Non-standard English** will be used in some aspects of everyday spoken language, and for more informal writing such as texting. It will often not be grammatically correct. For example, *'My friend don't like me anymore.'*

1 Decide which sentence in each pair is Standard English.

a	Here are the cakes what I bought.	Here are the cakes that I bought.
b	I don't want no ice cream.	I don't want any ice cream.
c	He walked so slowly.	He walked so slow.
d	I don't want no trouble.	I don't want any trouble.
e	Me and my friend went to the seaside.	My friend and I went to the seaside.
f	What are you staring at?	What you staring at?
g	They wanted it their selves.	They wanted it themselves.
h	Give me it back.	Give us it back.
i	The team played well.	The team played good.

2 Re-write these sentences in Standard English.
  a   I always write neat.
  b   She did good in the test.
  c   Arjan is more better at football than Sam.
  d   I didn't hardly survive.
  e   I never knew nothing.

Writing presentation

Write a text message to a friend, arranging to meet them after school. Write this in:
* Standard English
* Non-standard English.

I know about proverbs, sayings and figurative expressions.

Informal language

1 Change these informal, casual expressions into formal English. The first one has been done for you.

a Hi guys. *Hello everyone.*
b He chucked a pen at me.
c Winning the prize was really cool.
d You are out of your mind if you think that is going to happen.
e Are you going to dish out the sweets?

2 Proverbs are wise sayings that have been around for a long time. Their purpose is to provide us with a message we can apply to our own lives. Match the beginning of the proverb to the correct ending:

a	First come	is a friend indeed
b	More haste	first served
c	A friend in need	less speed
d	Practice	twice shy
e	No news is	has a silver lining
f	Every cloud	good news
g	One good turn	makes perfect
h	Once bitten	deserves another

Helpful hints

We use informal language in everyday speech. This type of language includes some words and expressions which are widely known and understood, but can sometimes be confusing for people new to learning the language. It should not be used in formal writing.

Here are some examples:

* It's raining cats and dogs.
  It is raining really hard.
* That computer costs an arm and a leg.
  The computer is expensive.
* The new game is mega.
  The new game is really good.
* All kids like chocolate.
  All children like chocolate.

Talk Partners

People sometimes make up sayings. These will be the expressions they use regularly on a daily basis amongst their family and friends. For example, 'Family is everything' or 'Don't worry, it might never happen.'

Share and write down some sayings that you know of with a partner. Agree on three or four which should be more widely known. Present these sayings to the rest of the class, explaining why.

I know the features of advertisements.

Advertisements

Here is an advertisement by WWF-UK. It aims to persuade the reader to adopt a snow leopard because they are in danger of becoming extinct.

Helpful hints

Advertisements are sometimes written as if the writer is speaking directly to the reader, so are more likely to use informal language. For example: *Feel like a holiday? You know it makes sense ... Go for it!*

Here are some other features writers of advertisements use to 'speak' to the reader:

- Personal pronouns, for example, you, me, us, our.
- Use of the apostrophe for contraction, for example, you'll.
- 'But' and 'And' often used at the beginning of sentences.
- Dashes to suggest the person has paused.
- Rhetorical questions.

WWF ADOPTION

ADOPT HIM TODAY.
OR LOSE HIM FOREVER.

Will you help the snow leopard claw its way back from the brink?

The Purrrfect gift!

Snow leopards have survived in the Himalayas for thousands of years. But right now, there are as few as 300 left in Nepal. The harsh reality is that they are being slaughtered by poachers for their bones and precious fur – and they urgently need your help if they are to live on.

By adopting a snow leopard today, you'll help protect this endangered big cat for future generations.

Your present. Their future.
For as little as £3 a month, you or your loved ones will receive an adoption pack, an adorable cuddly toy, and regular updates from people on the ground working tirelessly to help save the beautiful snow leopard.

What's more, you'll have the satisfaction of knowing you're helping to train and equip courageous anti-poaching rangers. And you'll discover what it takes – and how it feels – to help save a species.

 + + = *from just* **£3 a month** Adopt a snow leopard today, by filling in the form now, visiting wwfsnowleopard.com or calling 0845 200 2392

A gorgeous snow leopard toy   **an adoption pack**   **regular updates from the field**

Advertisement features

1 Read the advertisement on page 126. Each paragraph has a key message. An example is given below for paragraph 1. Copy the table below and fill in the key messages for paragraphs 2, 3 and 4 using notes.

	Notes
Paragraph 1	*Hardly any snow leopards left. Poachers responsible. Help needed from us.*
Paragraph 2	
Paragraph 3	
Paragraph 4	

2 The reader will receive a toy, an adoption pack and regular updates if they pay £3 a month. What other reason might persuade the reader to want to help the snow leopard?

3 Copy and complete the table to find these features in the text:

Type of feature	Examples
Personal pronoun	
Contraction	
Sentences beginning with 'And', 'But'	
Dash	
Rhetorical question	

4 Advertisements often use opposing ideas to make the message clear. For example, 'Adopt him today. Or lose him forever.' Find one other pair of opposites used in the text.

5 Why has the writer decided to make paragraph 2 so short? Choose one answer.
  a   There was not enough space.
  b   To interest the reader.
  c   To draw attention to the key message.
  d   To make the reader read on.

Language in advertisements

I know how to spell words with different letters but the same pronunciation.

Helpful hints

The advert on page 126 uses the words 'generation' and 'satisfaction'. Both endings of words have the same spelling. However, the 'shun' sound can use different combinations of letters, for example, education, mission.

1

a Sort these words into five columns so that the words in each column have the same ending:

> station reduction explosion passion discussion
> magician exclusion pollution contribution fiction institution revolution
> transfusion constitution optician extension mission fraction nation
> confusion direction education physician possession foundation
> session electrician demonstration politician attention

b Which ending is used for occupations?
c Which is the most common ending?

2

Advertisements need to choose language carefully so that each word has the right effect on the reader. Here is an extract from the advertisement on page 126:

> Snow leopards have survived in the Himalayas for thousands of years. But right now, there are as few as 300 left in Nepal. The harsh reality is that they are being <u>slaughtered</u> by poachers for their bones and <u>precious</u> fur – and they <u>urgently</u> need your help if they are to live on.

a Decide which of the three words underlined is a verb, adjective or adverb.
b Explain the effect of each word on the reader.
c Find another verb, adjective and adverb that has been used to create an effect on the reader.

3

The choice of nouns is important in an advertisement.
What is the impact of the advertisement using the nouns below:
a 'People on the ground' rather than 'workers'?
b 'Species' rather than 'snow leopards'?
c 'Updates' rather than 'leaflets'?

Writing an advertisement

 a Write an advertisement for one of the following:
- a package to adopt an endangered wild animal
- contributions to a local charity, for example, homelessness
- contributions to the school improvement fund.

Make sure you include the following in your advertisement:

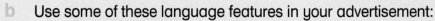

- Headline: Opposites followed by a rhetorical question
- Paragraph 1: Why the money is needed
- Paragraph 2: What the money will achieve in the future
- Paragraph 3: What a person's contribution will actually buy
- Paragraph 4: How a person's contribution will make them feel

b Use some of these language features in your advertisement:

- rhetorical question, for example, What hope is there?
- pronoun, for example, you, they, us
- precise nouns
- sentence started with 'But' or 'And'
- effective adverbs, for example, violently, peacefully, carefully

- emotive adjectives, for example, adorable, neglected, powerful
- dashes
- set of three, for example, No water, no food, no hope
- powerful verbs, for example, snatched, slaughtered.

Writing presentation

2 What image will you use to accompany your advertisement? The advertisement is of a serious nature so stick to two or three colours that are not too bright.

Use ICT to make your advertisement appear as if it has been produced professionally. For example, graphics, fonts, spacing. Make notes on how the 'snow leopard' advertisement has been laid out, and see how many features you can copy.

What have I learnt?

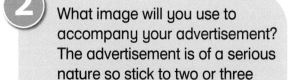

When you have completed the advertisement, use the list below to check that you have included:
- four paragraphs using the plan suggested, linking paragraphs together appropriately
- a speaking, conversational voice, for example, personal pronouns, sentences beginning with 'And'/'But', dashes, contractions (we'll), rhetorical questions
- language features, for example, set of three, powerful verbs, adjectives, and precise nouns
- a professional layout and presentation with colours sensibly used.

Unit 9 Suspense

I can structure talk to aid a listener's understanding and engagement.

I can vary vocabulary, expression and tone of voice so that I engage the listener.

Talk Partners

Share a frightening incident that happened to you with a partner. This should be an incident you **thought** was very frightening at the time, but ended happily. Use the three activities that follow to share your telling of the event in three different ways.

Helpful hints ⭐

We have all had frightening things happen to us at some point in our lives. These may have been quite minor, but won't have seemed so at the time! It might have been a coat hanging on a door that seemed to move, or hearing a strange noise. Our fears are often unfounded. It is our imagination. We **thought** something was there, and that something **might** happen.

1 Write what happened in three sentences. For example, 'It happened when I was six. I accidentally locked myself in the cupboard in my bedroom. I couldn't get out and it was really scary.'

2 Re-write and then re-tell the incident so that you stretch out what happened into five or six sentences. Don't give away the ending. For example:

'It was a rainy day and I was feeling quite bored. I had just seen a film about space travel, so thought it would be fun if I made the cupboard in my bedroom into a space room. I shut the door – really tightly – so I could pretend I was inside a real spaceship. It was so dark in the cupboard that at first I thought it was a bit like being in space. But after a while, I felt frightened. I tried to open the door, but it wouldn't open …

3 a Re-write and then re-tell the incident for a final time so you stretch it out into eleven or twelve sentences. Once again, do not give away the ending. Make sure you:
* Add information about smell, sound and touch.
* Include any voices as direct speech, for example, 'My mum called out to me'.
* Remember the 'show, not tell' rule. Make the listener **see** what made you frightened, for example, 'The darkness in the cupboard was as thick and black as the night sky.' Do not tell, for example, 'The cupboard was dark.'

b Which re-telling was more effective? Why?

Creating suspense

Read this extract from *Coraline* by Neil Gaiman.
Coraline is in bed when she hears a strange noise.

That night, Coraline lay awake in her bed. The rain had stopped, and she was almost asleep when something went t-t-t-t-t. She sat up in bed. Something went kreeee … … aaaak. Coraline got out of bed and looked down the hall, but saw nothing strange. She walked down the hallway. From her parents' bedroom came a low snoring – that was her father – and an occasional, sleepy mutter – that was her mother.

Coraline wondered if she'd dreamed it, whatever it was.

Something moved.

It was little more than shadow, and it scuttled down the darkened hall fast, like a patch of light.

She hoped it wasn't a spider. Spiders made Coraline intensely uncomfortable.

The black shape went in to the drawing room and Coraline followed it, a little nervously.

The room was dark. The only light came from the hall and Coraline, who was standing in the doorway, cast a huge and distorted shadow on the drawing room carpet: she looked like a thin giant woman.

Coraline was just wondering whether or not to turn on the light when she saw the black shape edge slowly out from beneath the sofa. It passed and then dashed silently across the carpet towards the farthest corner of the room.

Coraline turned on the light.

There was nothing in that corner. Nothing but the old door that opened to the back wall.

She was sure that her mother had shut the door, but now it was ever so slightly open. Just a crack. Coraline went over to it and looked in …

Adapted from Coraline by Neil Gaiman

How suspense is created

1

a Write four questions a reader might want answers to as they are reading the extract on page 131. For example, who is Coraline and where does she live?

b The writer has divided his writing into short paragraphs – with some being only one line long. This is done to create more suspense and tension. Copy out one short paragraph you found effective in creating suspense.

c Find three different ways the writer refers to the 'something' in the passage. (Hint: one other way is 'It'.)

d Why do you think the writer does not tell the reader what the 'something' is?

e The extract takes place late at night. How many references to dark and night can you find?

f If you were to meet Coraline, what type of person do you think she would be?

g Would you have opened the door to see what was behind it?

Helpful hints

What happens in the extract on page 131 is straightforward: Coraline is in bed, hears a noise and gets up to investigate it. However, the writer uses some clever techniques to create suspense and keep the reader's interest. After you have completed the activities on this page, you should be able to see what these are.

2 List the techniques the writer has used to create suspense.

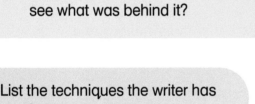

Talk Partners

Discuss your ideas with a talk partner on what Coraline might find when she opens the door. Agree on the best ideas, and then share these with another pair of talk partners.

Try this

Write the next paragraph of Coraline's story. Try to use as many suspense techniques as you can.

More suspense techniques

I know how to spot the mood of a story.

Night fell suddenly, and his heart beat fast. His throat went dry and he realized that he had not reached the **trunk road**. The trees were still thick and the road was still narrow. The trunk road was broader, and there the sky was not screened by branches. But here one could hardly see the sky; the stars gleamed through occasional gaps overhead. He quickened his pace though he was tired. He ran a little distance, his feet falling on the leaf-covered ground with a sharp rustling noise. The birds in the branches overhead started at this noise and fluttered their wings. In that deep darkness and stillness the noise of the fluttering wings had an **uncanny eerie quality**. Swaminathan was frightened and stood still. He must reach the trunk road and find his way home...

Extract from Swami and Friends by R. K. Narayan

Glossary

trunk road: a main road
uncanny: strange or mysterious
eerie: frightening
a quality: a characteristic possessed by someone or something

1

Read the extract above and answer these questions.

a At the beginning of the extract the writer suggests that the character is scared. Find two phrases which show this.

b List the things the character can hear in the extract. How does this add to the suspense?

c How does this phrase create suspense: 'the noise of the fluttering wings had an uncanny eerie quality'?

d Give one feature the reader finds out about the character during the extract.

e The extract finishes at a very tense point. What do you think might happen next?

Helpful hints

In the extract, the character is lost and trying to get home. The writer has given the reader a great deal of visual information about the setting and the character's actions. This adds to the suspense.

Comparing extracts

1 From your study of the two suspense extracts on pages 131 and 133, you will have learned some of the techniques used by writers to create suspense. Copy and complete the table below. You will need to read and refer to both extracts again.

Techniques for creating suspense	
Technique	**Example from the extracts**
Darkness	*'The room was dark'*
Sound	
A strange 'something/someone' suggested	
Hints about the character given through their movement and behaviour	
Cliff-hanger ending	

2 The writers of both extracts use visual details so that the reader can see what is happening. Copy and complete the table to find an example of one adjective, one verb and one short sentence in each extract that makes the reader **see** the detail.

Extract	Adjective	Verb	Short sentence
Coraline	<u>darkened</u> hall		
Swaminathan			

3 Writers will often use a simile to give more visual detail by comparing one thing to another. Similes always use 'like' or 'as'. For example, *The deserted house (one picture) was like an empty playground* (another picture).
   a   Which of the two extracts contains a simile?
   b   Copy out the simile and explain its effect.

4 a   Which extract do you prefer? Give a reason for your answer.
   b   Using your preferred extract, draw what the writer has described. Did you find it easy to do?

I can plan plot characters, setting and structure effectively.

I can establish and maintain a clear viewpoint when I am writing.

I can use the suspense genre as a model for writing.

Planning a suspense story

 1 Using the strategies you have learnt, you are going to write a suspense extract of your own. Here is the beginning of a story.

> *Slowly, with my hand trembling, I turned the handle of the old oak door...*

Plan the next part of the story, finishing at an exciting point for the reader. Have very little actually happening. Stretch out the story with description, an unexpected noise, the suggestion of something or someone. It is important that you don't give away the ending, and keep the reader in suspense. Use the diagram below to help you plan what is seen and heard in the room – and who or what might be there.

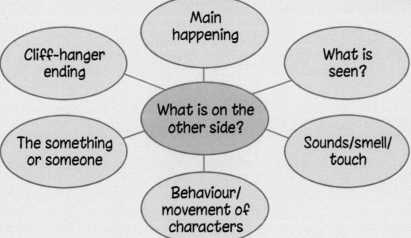

Main happening

Cliff-hanger ending

What is seen?

What is on the other side?

The something or someone

Sounds/smell/ touch

Behaviour/ movement of characters

2 Draw four or five boxes to represent the paragraphs in your story. Write your ideas from your plan in each one. Think hard about what order you want them to be in. Your cliff-hanger ending will obviously be at the end. Perhaps the beginning is a description of what is in the room, then a noise, then smell and touch, then more sound, then something moving …

Writing a suspense story

Read through this extract.

> The door banged. Aashif turned round, suddenly afraid. Who could it be? It wasn't Hamdi because he could be heard banging a football on the outside school steps, the noise echoing repetitively through the cold night air.
>
> Thud. Thud, Thud. The dull bang of heavy footsteps making their way along the long, empty corridor was unmistakable now.
>
> Somebody was coming closer. Somebody or something was coming down the corridor. Nearer and nearer. Aashif stood still, his shallow breath emerging in quick, jagged bursts. He made his way forward through the fading light of the empty classroom, soft and silent as a cat. Then he saw it. A dark shadow. Silently slipping out into the darkness of the long, unlit corridor, Aashif followed it …

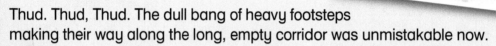

a Make a list of features that have been used to create suspense. You should be able to find at least six.

b Choose three features that are new to you and use them to improve your own suspense story.

Writing presentation

Using the plan from page 135, write the beginning to your suspense story, finishing at an exciting point. Remember to write in the first person, 'I … me … my …'

What have I learnt?

Read through your story and check that you have included all of the following features of the suspense genre. Put a tick next to each feature of your writing:

• darkness	• short sentences for effect	• small hints given about the character through their movement and behaviour
• touch		
• smell	• short paragraphs for effect	
• sound		
• adjectives and verbs used to show detail	• a strange 'something or someone' suggested	• cliff-hanger ending

Shades of meaning

I can explore definitions and shades of meaning and use new words.

1 Here are some words to do with suspense.
Pick the odd one out in each set.

a fear, terror, ache, alarm, dread, panic, horror
b dark, dim, shadowy, miserable, dusky, gloomy, black
c nervous, tense, solid, uneasy, anxious, jumpy, edgy
d sinister, ominous, forbidding, threatening, menacing, revolting

2 Match up these words with their synonyms in the cloud.

a ancient
b decaying
c empty
d silent

e cold
f vague
g echo

unclear

decrepit   old   noiseless

resonate   icy   bare

3 This extract has some words missing to do with fear, darkness and the unknown.
Put these back in the right place.

dark terror blackness mystery nervous

'You can do this,' he told himself, 'You can really do this.' But he hadn't convinced his body he could do this. His first attempt at tying the string to the door failed. He was so ... his fingers just wouldn't work. It was like wearing mittens and trying to knot raw sausages. Taking a deep, shuddering breath he finally managed to pass the string through the hatch and secure it to one of the little bars in the opening. He took his first faltering steps down the ... passageway. The ... clung to him, trying to crawl inside his skin.

The maze of tunnels was everything he had been expecting – and more. They had the ... of the night, the ... of loneliness. They lay deep beneath the earth, where the sun never shone and fresh wind never blew, and the silence was heavy.

Shadow of the Minotaur by Alan Gibbons

I can develop knowledge of word roots, prefixes and suffixes.

I know about different word endings which sound the same but are spelt differently.

I know how to transform meaning with prefixes.

Spelling rules for word endings and prefixes

1 Change these adjectives into nouns.

a distant → distance
b brilliant
c violent
d different
e obedient
f constant
g significant
h resistant
i obedient
j evident

Helpful hints

Adding a prefix or a suffix to a word will change its meaning.

im, ir, il, in are all prefixes which mean **not**. When words end in **ence** or **ance** it can be difficult to tell the difference as they both sound the same.

As a rule:
- Adjectives ending in **ant** can change to nouns ending in **ance**. For example, eleg**ant** → eleg**ance**
- Adjectives ending in **ent** can change to nouns ending in **ence**. For example, abs**ent** → abs**ence**

2 Another helpful rule to know is that when a prefix is added to a root word it will have an effect on whether there is a double letter or not, e.g. **im**proper, **in**active, **ir**responsible, **il**literate.
Add the prefix to each of these root words so that the spelling is correct.

im	in	il	ir
mature	decent	legal	responsible
mobile	convenient	logical	regular
practical	attentive	literate	rational
proper	credible	lustrous	resistible
possible	capable	legitimate	reparable

How characters show emotion in drama

Helpful hints

Playscripts are mainly about action and character – people talking and doing things.
- There is no need for lots of description. We can tell what is going on through what the characters say.
- The setting is important as it can affect the action. For example, the setting of a deserted house is very different from a busy, city street.
- Speech marks are not necessary in a play. The name of the character speaking is written in the left hand margin of the script.

Playwrights will often write down exactly how people speak.

Emir: I'm, um, not really, er, you know, s-s-s-sure ... what to ...

Adisa: I'm SO, SO excited!

Will: No – no. Don't go there. Please – don't …

- In a story, you can write about what someone is thinking. In a play, this is more difficult – although sometimes characters can speak their thoughts aloud. A good actor can suggest a lot through the expression on their face, the tone of their voice and how they say the words.

1 Read the playscript extract below. Re-write it so that you:
a show exactly how the characters speak
b add punctuation (dashes, ellipses, exclamation marks) to make the characters' speech convey feelings.

Scene: Old deserted shack
Characters: Shani (aged 12)
           Chimelu (aged 9)
The two children are walking towards the door. Shani is at the front. Chimelu is lagging behind, and seems reluctant.
Chimelu: I'm frightened. I don't want to go in.
Shani: Why are you crying? We agreed we should come here. You said you wanted an adventure.
(Door of shack swings open with a loud bang.)
Chimelu: I want to go home. I'm scared.
(An animal hoot is heard.)
Chimelu: Ooh
Shani: It's only the wind. We're going in. Follow me.

In the following short playscript extract, three children have gone back into their school in the evening to retrieve a jacket.

Talk Partners

Scene: School, early evening

Characters: Julieta, Ana, Jorge – all 10 years old
(Early evening. Outside the entrance of a school. It has started to rain, and the faint roll of thunder can be heard.)

Ana: *(pleadingly)* It won't take a minute. I've got to get it back. My mum will be so cross when she finds out I've left my brand new jacket behind. I need to get it back before tomorrow morning. PLEASE. Come into the school with me. You know I don't like the dark.
(She moves towards the entrance. The other two children hang back, reluctant.)

Ana: Come on, you PROMISED me you'd come. We've only got ten minutes. The caretaker locks everything up at eight o'clock.

Julieta: *(anxiously)* Say … he sees us?

Ana: He never comes before eight o'clock. The back of the school is always locked up first. Our classroom is at the front, remember?

Jorge: *(resigned)* I'm getting soaked. Let's do it.
(The children move slowly and apprehensively down the school corridor. The faint noise of thunder can be heard.)

Ana: Oooh … It's so dark with no lights on.
(They clutch one another's hands.)

Jorge: We're lucky the classroom has not been locked … It's so dark, I can't even see the desk and chairs.
(A loud thud.)

Julieta: What was that?

Ana: Can't we switch on the lights?
(Flash of lightning overhead.)

Ana: Did you hear that?

Julieta: What?

Jorge: There's someone coming!
(They all stop and listen.)

Jorge: *(whispering)* The door handle. Look! It's turning …

With your talk partner, perform two different versions of the play. In version 1, the lines should be delivered in a matter of fact way, with no emotion conveyed. The second version should show the full extent of the characters' feelings – showing more suspense.

2 Stage directions, sound effects and the characters' feelings are shown in brackets.

   a Sum up what happens in the play in three sentences.

   b Give three sound effects in the play.

   c Who do you think is going to come through the door? Write the ending of the play.

PRACTICE TEST 3

Fiction

Read the extract and answer the questions which follow.

This extract is from the short story by Anthony Horowitz, 'The Man With the Yellow Face'. A boy decides to get his photograph taken at a photo booth – a decision that will have great consequences for him in the future.

Was there something strange about that photo booth? It's easy enough to think that now, but maybe even then I was a little … scared. If you've been to York you'll know that it's got a proper, old station with a soaring roof, steel girders and solid red brickwork. The platforms are long and curve round, following the rails. When you stand there you almost imagine that a steam train will pull in.

But the photo booth was modern. It was an ugly metal box with its bright light glowing behind the plastic facings. It looked out-of-place on the platform – almost as if it had landed there from outer space. It was in a strange position too, quite a long way from the entrance and the benches where my uncle and aunt were sitting. You wouldn't have thought that many people would have come to this part of the platform. As I approached it, I was suddenly alone.

And maybe I imagined it, but it seemed that a sudden wind had sprung up, as if blown my way by an approaching train. I felt the wind, cold against my face.

But there was no train.

I pulled back the curtain and went into the photo booth. There was a circular stool which you could adjust for height and a choice of backgrounds – a white curtain, a black curtain, or a blue wall. The people who designed these things were certainly imaginative. I sat down and looked at myself in the square of black glass in front of me. This was where the camera was, but looking in the glass I could only vaguely see my face. I could make out an outline; my hair falling down over one eye, my shoulders, the open neck of my shirt. But my reflection was shadowy and, like the voice on the tannoy, distant. It didn't look like me.

'The Man with the Yellow Face' by Anthony Horowitz

1 Where does the story take place? (1)

2 Where is the photo booth situated?
   a railway station
   b street
   c shopping centre (1)

3 Give a quotation which shows that this incident happened in the past. (1)

4 Give three features that are strange about the photo booth. (3)

5 Give the meaning of the words underlined so that they mean the same as in the passage.

   a 'with a <u>soaring roof</u>, steel girders and solid red brickwork'

   b 'I could only <u>vaguely</u> see my face.'   (2)

6 The writer has created a number of narrative hooks which would make the reader want to read on. Give two.   (2)

7 Give one way the writer has used weather to suggest suspense. (1)

8 The writer suggests that the narrator is fading from normal life as the extract progresses. Give two quotations which show this. (2)

9 Give one contrast which is suggested in this extract. (1)

10 Choose the genre of the extract.
   a Real life adventure
   b Science fiction
   c Folk tale
   d Legend
   e Biography (1)

11 Whose point of view does the story focus on and how do we know this? (2)

12 Why is the paragraph 'But there was no train' so short? (1)